Secrets of
Personal Marketing Power

Strategies for Achieving Greater Personal and Business Success

Don L. Price

KENDALL/HUNT PUBLISHING COMPANY
4050 Westmark Drive   Dubuque, Iowa 52002

Copyright © 1994 by Don L. Price

ISBN 0-8403-9392-X

All rights reserved. No part of this publication may be reproduced, stored in a retrieval system, or transmitted, in any form or by any means, electronic, mechanical, photocopying, recording, or otherwise, without the prior written permission of the copyright owner.

Printed in the United States of America.
10 9 8 7 6 5 4 3 2 1

DEDICATION

This book is dedicated to all who have inspired and enriched my life through their love, encouragement and insight. To Keri and Kristy, of whom I'm so proud, and to my mother, who has a very giving and loving spirit.

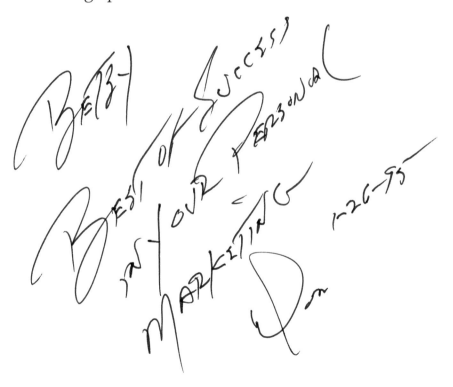

CONTENTS

Introduction, ***xi***

Part 1   Principles, 1

Chapter 1   Principles of Personal
            Marketing Power, **3**
   Success through luck, 3
   The first principle, 4
   The second principle, 6
   The third principle, 7
   The fourth principle, 10
   The fifth principle, 11
   Six smart action steps, 14

Chapter 2   Become a Miracle Maker, **17**
   Developing Your "Personal Marketing Power", 17

Chapter 3   Keys for Your Success, **23**
   Know who you are, 23
   Where do I want to go?, 24
   How will I get there?, 24
   Do I dare to dream?, 25
   Am I committed?, 25
   Your Personal Vision, 26
   Choosing "Personal Marketing Power", 28

Part 2　The Power of Networking, 31

Chapter 4　Your Center of Power, **33**
　　　Personal Marketing Secret #1, 33
　　　How Networking Drives the Center of Your Power

　　　Power Networking Golden Rules
　　　for Personal Success, 35
　　　　Active listening
　　　　Asking smart questions
　　　　Power group presentations
　　　　Relationship building
　　　　Personal visibility
　　　　Mastering networking protocol
　　　　Business cards
　　　　Notes of appreciation
　　　　Professional presence
　　　　Follow-up
　　　　Stay connected with people

Part 3　Powers that Influence, 47

Chapter 5　The Magic Power of Influence, **49**

Chapter 6　More Secret Weapons of
　　　　　"Personal Marketing Power", **51**
　　　Personal Marketing Secret #2, 52
　　　Activate Your Creative Powers
　　　to Open Doors of Opportunity

Chapter 7　Power Weapons that Position You
　　　　　as an Expert, **55**

Personal Marketing Secret #3, 55
Marketing with Newsletters
Builds Image & Credibility

Personal Marketing Secret #4, 60
How to Get Your Customer to Pay for
Your Marketing With Audio Newsletters
& Audio Magazines

Personal Marketing Secret #5, 62
Get Published in Other Newsletters

Personal Marketing Secret #6, 65
Build & Pump-up Your Career with News Articles
    The secret is out—getting writers
        to write about you

Personal Marketing Secret #7, 72
Be A Self-Promotion Personal Marketing Maverick
    Selling your topic to the media
    Media tips for a promising and
        successful promotion

Personal Marketing Secret #8, 75
Think Innovatively about TV Talk Shows

Personal Marketing Secret #9, 76
Power-up Your Career by Writing Your First Book
    Your Road to having Your Book Published

Personal Marketing Secret #10, 78
How Teaching an Adult Education Class is Often
Overlooked as a Smart Personal Marketing Concept

Personal Marketing Secret #11, 80
Projecting Your Image of Excellence

Personal Marketing Secret #12, 83
Why Photo Business Cards are Important
and How You Profit from Them
> They Won't Let Go—Your Business Card
> Puts Cash in Their Pockets
> Use Other Peoples' Business Cards for Your Own
> Personal Marketing

Personal Marketing Secret #13, 86
> Stay Well Connected With People Using
> Photo Post Cards

Part 4 The Power of Simple Truth, 91

Chapter 8 Simple Truths in Getting People to Believe in You, **93**

Personal Marketing Secret #14, 93
Letting Others Blow Your Horn
with Testimonial Letters

Personal Market Secret #15, 95
Referrals—The Influential Power of People

Personal Market Secret #16, 98
How Smart Marketers Get Free Publicity
by Endorsing Other Peoples' Products

Personal Marketing Secret #17, 99
Fast Forward Your Career by Speaking to Groups
> Know where to speak to advance your
> self-promotional personal marketing objectives
> Getting invited

Personal Marketing Secret #18, 104
Promote Your Product, Company And Service With
Seminars And Workshops
    The magic marketing rule of success

Personal Marketing Secret #19, 108
Thank You Notes and Letters Build Lasting and
Powerful Relationships

Personal Marketing Secret #20, 109
Your Marketing Kit is Your Top Coat to Success

Part 5　More Power Weapons, 115

Chapter 9　Smart Ideas That Work, 117
Personal Marketing Secret #21, 117
The Power of Unsolicited Testimonials

Personal Marketing Secret #22, 120
Help Support Your Customers' Cause

Personal Marketing Secret #23, 121
Shrewd Marketing with Video Brochures

Personal Marketing Secret #24, 122
Audio Brochures Put You on the
Leading Edge of Your Industry

Personal Marketing Secret #25, 124
Use Team Marketing for Propelling
Your Business to Greater Success

Personal Marketing Secret #26, 125
Personalized Information Letters—Staying Well-
Connected to Your Customers Brings Profits

Chapter 10 Put Your Mind To Work On Creativity,
Imagination And Innovation, **127**

Part 6   Your Power Plan, 131

Chapter 11 Building Your
"Personal Marketing Power", **133**
First things first, 133
Embody passion, insight and vision, 135
Time to take inventory, 136
Masterminding your Personal Marketing plan, 139
Building a bigger network
Your personal marketing campaign
Is a book in your future plans?
Your marketing team
Organize and evaluate
Stepping into your plan of action, 142

Appendix, **145**

Index, **155**

INTRODUCTION

Someone asked me why I was writing a book on Personal Marketing Power. My answer was startlingly simple, and based on insights and observations about how people and companies were becoming wealthy in the 90's. In today's increasingly complex, competitive and challenging marketplace you must learn to live with a steady diet of change and innovation, in order to achieve success in your career and business. The idea of working hard, having drive, determination and a positive mind set, doesn't seem to fit the mood of the decade. I have learned over the years that those are all great attributes to possess, but, by themselves, won't carry you to your golden destination. It wasn't until after many years of trying to figure out the elusive secret that enabled others to achieve business success, that I found the real secret to producing incredible results in business. The secret is in marketing—personal marketing.

You can't possibly fulfill your dreams without having the knowledge and wisdom to personally market yourself. Knowledge is the information and know-how necessary to accomplish a goal. Wisdom is the enlightenment which will maximize and optimize opportunity. In order to optimize your opportunities you must first identify all of your assets, relationships and networking channels. Most importantly you must recognize the value and significant roles other people play in contributing to your success. You need to look seriously at the biggest obstacles that prevent you from making things happen. Making the right assumptions about what this world is all about will be your best guidepost for knowing when to be optimistic or pessimistic about your future plans. However, I find that most self-imposed obstacles, to someone fulfilling their dreams, are not necessarily optimism or pessimism as procrastination and fear. Procrastination and fear kill off more dreams, drown the eternal flame of hope and stop people short of finding optimal success and happiness. You must be passionate and have a creative vision about what it is you do and what it is you want. Most of all you must be innovative in your marketing strategies and your marketing tools to show others the advantages you offer.

More than anything else, marketing is the secret to achieving great business success and financial freedom. You must understand that out-marketing your competition is your one guarantee of both a bright future and a prosperous enterprise.

I have endeavored to present in this book some of the most powerful personal marketing tools available for those who would like to take a quantum jump in their careers and business growth. This book is for people who want to stay competitive, create a professional presence and make a difference.

Any person in any industry can benefit from the simple and innovative personal marketing ideas presented in this book. If you are in real estate, mortgage lending, insurance, politics; a professional speaker, writer, consultant, fund raiser, social activist, business owner, professional, personal fitness trainer, or anyone who wants to master their personal marketing and create an edge for market dominance and financial rewards, then read this book to learn the secrets of personal marketing power for increasing your success and value in the marketplace.

Part One
PRINCIPLES

CHAPTER 1 Principles of Personal
Marketing Power

CHAPTER 2 Become a Miracle Maker

CHAPTER 3 Developing Your Own
"Personal Marketing Power"

CHAPTER

1

PRINCIPLES OF PERSONAL MARKETING POWER

Success Through Luck

Someone once said "When all is said and done—there is more said than ever done." However, there are those few rare exceptions who forge persistently and courageously ahead to accomplish their goals and aspirations, and seemingly do so with little effort. Many would call them lucky. Or some would say that they were fortunate enough to be in the right place at the right time, or that they are lucky because they were born that way. In the traditional American success story, luck has always played a significant role. To a remarkable degree, I personally believe people do indeed make their own luck, in the sense that their knowledge, know-how and ambition to get ahead positioned them in the right place and at the right time for luck to strike.

Secrets of Personal Marketing Power

> "Luck can often mean simply taking advantage of a situation at the right moment. It is possible to make your luck by being always prepared."[1]

Whatever reason people give for others' success—call it lucky or happenstance—I'm convinced that those individuals created their own luck. They did it simply by developing their innate sense of "Personal Marketing Power."

That's exactly what you will be able to do—create your own luck by developing your own "Personal Marketing Power." That's what this book is all about.

Whether you're looking for a new job, climbing the corporate ladder, or selling your services, products, or ideas, understanding what "Personal Marketing Power" is and how to effectively apply its principles will be the magical key that unlocks the door to your personal success.

Contrary to popular belief, building your "Personal Marketing Power" doesn't require that you have a marketing degree from a prestigious, top ten business university, or that you have extensive experience from working for a Madison Avenue marketing or public relations firm.

What it does require is that you understand and apply the principles and "Secrets of Personal Marketing Power"—principles and secrets that have worked successfully for all who use them.

The First Principle

"IT'S WHO YOU KNOW AND WHO KNOWS YOU THAT BRINGS YOU SUCCESS IN LIFE!"

Let me repeat that again. "It's who you know and who knows you that brings you success in life!" The old traditional attitudes and

[1] Michael Korda, *Success*, page 35, Random House, 1977.

Chapter 1

notions about working harder, believing in yourself and always thinking positively are not good enough for climbing the ladder of success. I've seen people who worked hard all their lives, sometimes sixteen hours a day. They believed in themselves and were positive thinkers, only to end up retired with little more to show for than when they first started out in life. Don't misunderstand me. There is nothing wrong with working hard and thinking positively; however, that's only part of the formula to success.

> "Thousands of geniuses live and die undiscovered—either by themselves or by others." *Mark Twain*

In today's business world, genius is found in successful people who look to others to help make them successful. You, too, have to look to others for your success. How do you get others to help make you successful? You go out and boldly market yourself.

The principles are demonstrated everyday though the success of everyone around us. We can take a lesson from Harvey Mackay who wrote his first book at the age of 54. *Swim With The Sharks Without Being Eaten Alive* broke all sorts of publishing records. Over 2.3 million copies sold and it remained on the *New York Times* bestseller list (of business titles) for more than 40 weeks, ranking among the ten top-selling business titles of all time. Mackay now enjoys the fruits of his success as a popular business speaker, with two additional books to his credit.

In my estimation, Harvey Mackay will always be one of the top marketing mavericks of this decade. There is no question in my mind that Harvey Mackay recognized the value of others' testimonials to position the dynamic overnight success of *Swim With The Sharks Without Being Eaten Alive*.

I believe he knew that for the book to be a bestseller he had to look to others for his success. He obtained some of the best endorsements available. The list of endorsements included celebrities, CEO's, major newspapers and other notables such as:

The Reverend Billy Graham
Larry King, of *Larry King Live*
The late Dr. Norman Vincent Peale

Secrets of Personal Marketing Power

Joan Lunden, co-host of ABC-TV's *Good Morning America*
USA TODAY
NEWSWEEK
Peter V. Ueberroth, then Commissioner of Baseball
The Wall Street Journal
Fran Tarkenton—famed quarterback of the Minnesota
    Vikings
Denis Waitley—Best-selling author of *The Psychology of
    Winning*
Ted Koppel, of ABC-TV's *Nightline*
Lou Holtz, Head Football Coach, University of Notre Dame
Gerald R. Ford, former President
Stephen Wolf, Chairman and CEO, United Airlines

With that line-up, I believe Harvey Mackay could have written a book on "How To Mow The Grass With Ten Inches Of Snow On It" and still have had a best seller. The point is that if you were lucky enough and had that kind of power supporting you with endorsements, you would have a best-selling book also.

That brings us to our second principle of "Secrets of Personal Marketing Power."

The Second Principle

"YOUR SUCCESS COMES FROM MOBILIZING THE POWER OF OTHERS"

Throughout the ages great leaders, musicians, artists, athletes, salespeople, writers, politicians and even gangsters, dictators, and monarchs, have all established their positions of power though others.

According to *Your Company*, a business resource magazine published by American Express, partners Jonathan Carson and Carroll Miller started Educational Publishing Group, Inc. in Boston. Jonathan and Carroll publish an educational newsletter

6

Chapter 1

for parents about children's education. They had successfully found their marketing niche for the newsletter. However, sales from subscriptions were disappointing and things seemed to be going nowhere fast. At about this point, they felt they could take the business in only two directions. They could either slow down and re-group or go full steam ahead by obtaining more capital. Then came a turning point. Several major corporations placed large subscription orders. But more importantly, they were able to mobilize the power of their friends and others. They gained credibility and cultivated many contacts after a mutual friend introduced Jonathan to former Massachusetts Senator Paul Tsongas. Jonathan immediately recruited Tsongas to sit on his board of advisers. From the publicity that followed and the new orders, their Educational Publishing Group took a quantum leap, putting their young enterprise on a successful path.[2]

> "Whatever you do, try to stay as physically close to the center of power as possible."[3]

Remember the old saying, "Out of sight, out of mind. Out of mind, out of luck."? Well, if you want to be in luck, you must be in mind and to be in mind you must be in sight, thus putting you close to the center of your power—which is that other people can push or pull you to your success. That brings us to our third principle and "Secret Of Personal Marketing Power."

The Third Principle

"LUCK AND OPPORTUNITY WILL PRESENT ITSELF TO THOSE WHO MAKE PERSONAL MARKETING THEIR MISSION."

---

[2]From *Your Company*, Published by American Express Publishing Corporation, exclusively for American Express Corporate Cardmembers.
[3]Al Ries, Jack Trout, *Horse Sense*, page 145, Plume, 1992.

7

Secrets of Personal Marketing Power

> **"The only way to convert a heathen is to travel into the jungle."** *Lane Kerland*

When you have decided to make "Personal Marketing" your mission and position yourself for greater success, you will begin to literally forge ahead into a jungle, taking massive controlled actions to get as many supporters in your camp as possible. However, for most therein lies the problem—taking massive action. You must ask for what you want. It sounds simple. But the truth is, people seldom ask for what they want. If you are to succeed you must not ask for what you think you can get or what you think is reasonable. You must be unreasonable in your demands.

> **"Never limit yourself to what you think is reasonable or possible. You have to learn that ambition and desires may seem more unreasonable to you than they do to other people."**[4]

Remember this—the sudden leap to success and wealth seldom comes through the normal channels. Asking for, and getting what you want will be entirely up to you. You are the product, and your goal and objective is to get your head above the pack and be seen, and to recognize and take advantage of opportunity and luck when it comes along.

The more you take advantage of opportunity the luckier you get. Marshall Johnson is a good example. Johnson and a friend were discussing the absence of African/American figures on U.S. currency. Another friend suggested putting historical African/Americans on bank checks. Being innovative, Marshall Johnson took the idea and developed the African/American Heritage check series. Johnson then went through a series of marketing strategies to launch his company. One of the tactics he used was to offer an exclusive market area to several banks that would introduce the checks to their customers. Also he negotiated a licensing agreement with Deluxe Check Printers in Shoreview,

---

[4]Michael Korda, *Success*, page 44, Random House, 1977.

8

Chapter 1

Minnesota. Deluxe controls about half the U.S. market for printing personal checks. However, when Deluxe and Johnson were negotiating the printing contract, Deluxe—being doubtful about the success of Johnson's African/American Heritage Check Series—failed to sign an exclusive licensing agreement. Here another lucky opportunity presented itself to Johnson. How lucky for Johnson? Deluxe's lack of vision gave Johnson the opportunity to sign agreements with three other major printers, giving his African/American Heritage Check Series nearly blanket coverage of the banking industry. Johnson has a ways to go—maybe he'll get even luckier by hitching onto a celebrity endorsement.[5]

> **"Luck is the sense to recognize an opportunity and the ability to take advantage of it. Everyone has bad breaks, but everyone also has opportunities. The man who can smile at his breaks and grab his chance gets on."**
> *Samuel Goldwyn*

My dear friend Barbara Wold, professional speaker, business consultant and author of the *Yearbook* is a person who has recognized her lucky opportunities in pursuit of her dream. The *Yearbook* was designed to be a yearly planner for the retail industry. However, as fate or luck would have it, Barbara soon discovered through her own insights as, well as those of her friends, that the *Yearbook* had incredible application in almost any industry. All Barbara would have to do was redesign the content of the *Yearbook*, not the concept or application. Therefore, Barbara had in her hands a multi-million dollar opportunity and product if marketed correctly. Barbara began listing all the potential industries, and companies within those industries, which she felt would see the value of her product. Determining which companies to target for her *Yearbook*, Barbara then set out to contact each one. Through her networking with friends and associates Barbara is currently making inroads in several national as well as international companies, all of which may not have come about had Barbara not recognized her opportunity.

---

[5]From *Your Company*, published by American Express Publishing Corporation, exclusively for American Express Corporate Cardmembers.

Secrets of Personal Marketing Power

Recognizing an opportunity and acting on it, in many situations, is the lucky break we all seek in our careers and life.

The Fourth Principle

"BECOME A POWER NETWORKER"

We can all learn a great deal from the message of Robert Muller, former Assistant Secretary-General of the United Nations:

> "Use every letter you write, every conversation you have, every meeting you attend to express your fundamental beliefs and dreams. Affirm to others the vision of the world you want. Network through thought. Network through love. Network through the spirit. You are the center of the network. You are the center of the world. You are a free, immensely powerful source of life and goodness. Affirm it, spread it, radiate it. Think day and night about it and you will see a miracle happen: the greatness of your own life. Not in a world of big powers, media and monopolies, but of five and a half billion individuals. Networking is the new freedom, the new democracy, a new form of happiness."
> *Robert Muller*

Donna & Sandy Vilas, in their book *Power Networking*, note that "Networking creates a power that leads to a richer, fuller personal and professional life. When we speak of "Power" networking we mean a power that comes from a spirit of giving and sharing.[6]

Joe Griffith—author and speaker—says, "Innovation doesn't always mean spending big money."[7] He spoke about a cosmetics

---

[6]Donna & Sandy Vilas, *Power Networking*, Mountain Harbour, page 15, 1992.
[7]Joe Griffith, *Speaker's Library of Business Stories, Anecdotes and Humor*, page 166, Prentice Hall, 1990.

Chapter 1

company needing a package for a new product. Designing it can be very costly, but at "Revlon, a new package was not designed, but innovated. A bottle was needed for *Jontue*, and some innovator saw that if the *Charlie* bottle was turned around it, looked like an entirely different package.

The Fifth Principle

"BE CREATIVE AND INNOVATIVE IN YOUR MARKETING"

About innovation: "If you see in any given situation only what everybody else can see, you can be said to be so much a representative of your culture that you are a victim of it."
S.I. Hayakawa

Creativity and innovation can open new opportunities in marketing you and your business.

No matter what the market conditions are, you need to position yourself in the marketplace correctly to maintain a high level of production. To do so requires having a plan of action that is innovative and creative to maintain an ongoing flow of quality leads and referrals for developing new business.

However, most individuals make bad decisions on how to develop market presence and position themselves in the marketplace. By positioning, I mean creating an innovative and tactical campaign that defines your role in the marketplace as an expert and the best in your industry.

For instance, in the mortgage industry some loan originators prefer using alternative documentation and thus specialize in fast funding. Quick turnaround, therefore, is their position in the marketplace. However, in today's marketplace, fast funding and quick turnaround may not be a good enough position in the

Secrets of Personal Marketing Power

market place. A tactical campaign of letting borrowers know specifically why it's smart to do business with them will have a greater impact.

Whatever marketing tools the loan originator uses should then get that message across. The role of marketing is to deliver those messages in a highly creative approach that is distinctive and compelling.

All of this may sound obvious, however most loan originators use the same old "me, too" marketing slogans as everyone else—

"We have lots of programs to choose from."
"We offer great service."
"Call us for the lowest rates."

By being that general and trying to appeal to a wide mass audience, many originators come across as just another loan agent in the industry. Few will remember their messages.

In today's highly competitive and creative marketplace, we must choose our marketing, and have it be very targeted. Let me give you my simple definition of marketing, broken down into two stages.

- Marketing is the process that favorably positions your company, product or service in the mind of the customer and is aimed at stimulating a desire and demand on the part of the customer.
- Personal marketing is the process that favorably positions you in the mind of the customer and is aimed at stimulating the customer to select you as the person from which they purchase.

One of our most cost-effective marketing strategies is developing a strong referral base of satisfied customers who spread the word to friends and family members. Nothing could be more targeted than that. And it will happen faster if you have developed your "Personal Marketing Power." With this quality you will stand out, rather than appearing to be just another "me, too" in your industry.

Your "Personal Marketing Power" is developed by mobilizing all of your mental and physical resources to effectively self-promote and position yourself favorably in the market place.

Chapter 1

"Personal Marketing Power" means that you will develop a unique approach to telling others what you do.

You need to market boldly and creatively. Again, it's important to be very specific in order to position yourself. The example of the loan originator may be one who might offer dozens of loan types. However, that person's target audience will remember them best if they see them as an expert in one area.

Instead of telling how many lenders with which they have been approved, positioning themself as a person who gets results in their loan specialty will yield greater results.

Be so compelling in your marketing that your prospects and customers will remember you as a person upon whom they could rely and want to be associated with in doing business, as well as referring business to you. To get started in marketing, capitalize on what your company does best, and what you are good at doing. Marketing encompasses a variety of activities simultaneously. How well you market yourself will depend on your time and money, and what tactics and strategic marketing tools you feel comfortable using. Here are just a few tools and ideas you can begin to use for marketing yourself:

- Personalized newsletters
- Testimonial letters
- Photo business cards and post cards
- Audio and video "brochures" on yourself
- Toll-free hotline
- Speaking before neighborhood groups, local clubs and associations
- Workshops and seminars
- Articles written about yourself
- Writing articles for publications in your industry
- Marketing kits (your promotional package)
- Join associations and civic clubs
- Sit on a board of directors or an advisory board
- Join a lead club
- Power networking
- Trade shows
- Endorsement of others or products
- Be interviewed on radio
- Write a book

Secrets of Personal Marketing Power

Marketing takes patience. But consider it an investment, not an expense. Photo business cards are more expensive, but studies show that four out of five traditional business cards are tossed out within half an hour after the salesperson has left.

Photo business cards reduce that frightening statistic, by making you more memorable.

Personalized newsletters are available, which are professionally written to suit your readers' needs. When you discover the value of newsletter marketing—specifically customer service newsletters—the benefits are enormous. Having an authoritative newsletter sets you apart as an expert. Show appreciation to customers by writing personalized hand-written letters and post cards. Your follow-up will be appreciated, and the rewards will follow with referrals.

"Personal Marketing Power" is a series of logical steps which can transform your business by building a pipeline of referrals and supporters—no matter what the market conditions.

Six Smart Action Steps

Here are six smart decisions and actions to take in your marketing:

1. Develop a passion for marketing and make it your mission. Communicate your own, and your company's, message in new, innovative, interesting and creative ways.
2. Let people know what they should think of you and your company. People draw conclusions by making comparisons—make sure they draw the right conclusions and make the right comparisons that will best serve your goals.
3. Focus on what your customers want, need, care about and expect from you.
4. Be relentless in your personal marketing—develop a maverick attitude. Persistence is power. Never let up on the tension of marketing. Many people never stay with anything long enough to produce results
5. Take advantage of testimonials. Your credibility increases if you let a satisfied customer blow your horn for you.

Chapter 1

6. Be creative and innovative. Today, it takes a highly creative and innovative approach to be distinctive and compelling.

> **"Personal Marketing Power" is to your success what the "Solid Rocket Motor" is to the space shuttle. It's the energy force and power lift system within you.** *Don L. Price*

Your "Personal Marketing Power" is something you develop daily, weekly, monthly and yearly through planning and setting specific goals.

CHAPTER

2

BECOME A MIRACLE MAKER

Developing Your
Personal Marketing Power

Through planning and setting goals individuals can create miracles. It's miracles that you create through effectively developing your "Personal Marketing Power." How you go about developing "Personal Marketing Power" has much to do with how you feel about yourself. This would include your self-esteem, your know-how, your education and the belief in yourself. In one of my "Personal Marketing Power" seminars that I presented in New Haven, Connecticut a young man stood up and, in a very forthright manner, said (as a matter of fact he was more than forthright) that it takes courage, self confidence and good self-esteem to put yourself in front of the public—and how right he is. It takes a lot of courage, self-confidence and a healthy self-esteem, all required characteristic traits. Also important are your attitudes about money, the economy, time and your personal desires.

In his book *Learned Optimism* author Martin Seligman, Ph.D. talks about traditional wisdom:

Secrets of Personal Marketing Power

> "That traditional wisdom holds that there are
> two ingredients of success, and you need both
> to succeed. The first is ability or aptitude
> and the second is desire or motivation.
> Traditional wisdom also holds that no matter
> how much aptitude you have, if you lack desire
> you will fail. Enough desire can make up
> for meager talent."

However, Seligman takes it one step further. He believes that traditional wisdom is incomplete.

> "Success requires persistence, the ability to not
> give up in the face of failure."[1]

Seligman's research validates that a successful person needs three characteristics—aptitude, motivation and optimism. Seligman doesn't advocate that optimism be applied blindly. He suggests that learning to be a flexible optimist will increase your control over the way you think about life's adversities. After studying Seligman's research, I'm firmly convinced that a pessimist doesn't have a chance on God's earth to develop a strong "Personal Marketing Power" profile simply because they think of ways for things to not work, whereas an optimist thinks in ways for things to work. It's in the optimistic stage that you employ your "Personal Marketing Power." It's in the optimistic stage that you influence others to champion your cause.

Les Brown, motivational speaker and author of *Live Your Dreams*, tells the story of when he hungered to be on radio as a disc jockey. He epitomized optimism, never looking at rejection as defeat. When Les walked into the radio station and approached the program manager for a job, he was turned down for lack of experience and was told, "We don't have a job for you." Les thanked the program manager and left, only to return the next day. Every day Les would return to the radio station asking for a

---

[1]Martin E.P. Seligman, Ph.D., *Learned Optimism*, page 101, Pocket Books, 1991.

Chapter 2

job and every day Les was told, "You're wasting your time." Nevertheless, he would say "thank you" and return the next day. Finally, persistence and optimism paid off for Les—he was hired as the radio station's errand boy on the fifth day. Les then became the best student he could, understudying everyone and studying everything so that when the day came for his opportunity, he was prepared to step in as a disc jockey.

Throughout the process, Les was positioning and personally marketing himself gaining others' trust, and being recognized for the talents and determination which enabled him to be the disc jockey he was so optimistic about becoming.

> "Your success is determined not by what you do, but rather by what you cause other people to do."[2]

Being an optimist, you are significantly different in that you cause others to react optimistically.

- If you are jockeying for position in your company, optimism is used to encourage others to rally to your support.
- If you are running for political office you'll need to inspire others to make them vote for you.
- If you are selling and promoting a product or service, competing in an athletic event or developing your "Personal Marketing Power" then you must have absolute unconditional optimism to succeed and be a winner.

Ask yourself the following questions: Just what is it that I want to accomplish in life? Do I have a majestic desire, and a passion for succeeding and turning my dreams into reality? What is my mission in life? Am I optimistic or pessimistic about life? Am I a doer in life or one who just sits, viewing my wish screen in my mind ? Can I accept the help of others or am I a "must do it myself" type of person? How you answer these questions could have a phenomenal impact on the extent and the degree to which you succeed in developing your "Personal Marketing Power." It's

[2]David J. Schwartz, *The Magic of Getting What You Want*, page 61, Berkeley, 1984.

Secrets of Personal Marketing Power

been my experience that most people apply their own brakes in life when it comes to fulfilling their true potential. People have all kinds of reasons for not succeeding. It's easier for them to put the responsibility of their failures outside of their control—meaning that they view their failures as due to circumstances beyond their power and control.

How many times have you destroyed your own dreams of going into business for yourself, or competing in an athletic event, or making a change in your career because you harbored the following thoughts:

- I don't have enough education.
- I lack the money to fund my project.
- I'm too young.
- The field is overcrowded.
- I don't have the time.
- The economy is bad.
- My parents wouldn't approve of it.
- I'm not talented enough.
- I'm not athletic.
- I fear others won't approve of my activity.

Harboring those thoughts in your mind will do nothing more that set you up for failure in life. However, the lessons of history and thousands of success stories will validate that rarely are these statements acceptable reasons for failing in life. Ray Kroc, founder of McDonald's Burgers at age fifty-two, could have said: "I'm too old" or "I don't have enough time left at my age to create a billions dollar empire." Fran Tarkenton, the famed quarterback of the Minnesota Vikings, could have used the excuse that he was too short. Bill Gates, founder of Microsoft, could have used the excuse that he was too young to be at the helm of a multi-billion dollar corporation. Such excuses had no power over these individuals in venturing out in pursuit of their passion and dreams. These excuses should have no power over you accomplishing your dreams.

Winning is our inherent right. In the pursuit of our dreams, we all have the potential ability to make winning a habit. Unfortunately, many have a steady diet of making losing their habit.

Chapter 2

Les Brown, author of *Live Your Dreams* and a motivational speaker, said that:

> "If you don't develop the hunger and courage to pursue your goal, you will lose your nerve and you will give up on your dream. If you don't have the courage to act, life will take the initiative from you."[3]

Act on life or risk having life act on You.

Winning means simply that you act on life. You set up your goals. Develop a plan of action to obtain your goals. You then reach and accomplish your goals. No matter how small or large the goal is, the fact that you set out and accomplished your goal means you have won. Developing your "Personal Marketing Power" is winning. For some, developing their "Personal Marketing Power" will require more courage to act on than it will for others. However, the more you act to develop your "Personal Marketing Power" the more opportunities you'll have to create a better paying job, sell more products, position yourself as an expert in your field, build a better speaking business, build a more profitable home-based business, or get yourself voted into office.

---

[3]Les Brown, *Live Your Dreams*, page 51, Morrow, 1992.

CHAPTER

3

KEYS FOR YOUR SUCCESS

Here are some keys for accomplishing your Personal Marketing Goals and questions to ask yourself. As you read, give serious thought as to how you would truly answer them. Even if you have gone through exercises or have answered similar questions before, don't be too quick to judge them or yourself. With a pencil or pen and notebook in your hands or sitting in front of your computer, take the time now to do a thorough check-up of yourself. Be brutally honest with yourself.

> "Whosoever knows others is clever. Whosoever knows himself is wise."   *Lao Tzu*

Knowing yourself is a smart and wise thing when it comes to guiding yourself through the journey of life.

- Know who you are. Ask questions like: What are my strengths and weaknesses? Make a personal assessment of yourself and be objective. Identify your skills and aptitudes in areas that you enjoy. For example, you like the fanfare and excitement of being the chairperson at

Secrets of Personal Marketing Power

one of your organizational or association meetings, you excel at it, and that is where you shine. However, you disdain all the details required of you. Because of the details it derails you from pursuing one of your "Personal Marketing Goals." Are you one who applies the brakes and stops short of your goal, or do you find creative solutions and move on? Are you someone who is always aiming for perfection and yet never quite master it, stopping you dead in your tracks and keeping you from accomplishing your goals?

> "Aiming for perfections is always a goal in progress."   *Thomas J. Watson Jr., IBM*[1]

So let perfection grow but don't let it sabotage your goals.

- Ask yourself: "Where do I want to go?" Will the direction in which you are moving get you to where you want to go in life? Are you running on a track that will help you realize your dreams, your vision, your "Personal Marketing Power" goals? If not, you had better find out quickly what course of action it will take to get you to where it is you want to go.

> "The greatest thing in this world is not so much where we are, but in what direction we are moving."   *Oliver Wendell Holmes*

- Ask yourself: "How will I get there?" Have you developed the characteristics and habits of a winner? Stephen R. Covey wrote in his book *The 7 Habits of Highly Effective People* that habits "have tremendous gravity pull—more than most people realize or would admit. Breaking deeply imbedded habitual tendencies such as procrastination,

---

[1]Quoted in *Speaker's Library of Business Stories, Anecdotes and Humor*, Joe Griffith, page 133.

Chapter 3

impatience, criticalness, or selfishness that violate basic principles of human effectiveness involves more than a little willpower and a few minor changes in our lives."[2] Do you have the habits of a winner that propels you toward achieving your "Personal Marketing Goals"? Do you have that burning desire, that cliff-hanging passion, and that absolute unconditional optimism, or are your habits of procrastination, impatience, and criticalness so "deeply imbedded" that they set up insurmountable road blocks? People who know where they want to go will know how to get there. Steven Jobs, founder of Apple Computer, knew exactly where he was going. It has been said that he was so sure of his direction at the age of twelve that he called Bill Hewlett, founder of Hewlett-Packard, and asked Bill if he would give him some computer parts to work with—the rest is history.

- Ask yourself: "Do I dare to dream?" Do you have a vision of your future? Dreams are the mental images we create in the privacy of our minds. They are our private screening of the world in which we would like to live. Our very own fantasies to orchestrate. We are the writer, director, and actor, editor, sound person, and critic. Our dreams can be real or imagined. It's all up to the dreamer. Dreams are the mental images of your goals, and your goals give you a vision that keeps you pressing on in life.

- Ask yourself: "Am I ready and willing to make a total commitment to my "Personal Marketing Power" goals?"

> "Commitment unlocks the doors of imagination, allows vision and gives us the 'right stuff' to turn our dreams into reality."
> *James Womack* [3]

Commitment is what gives you power, what guarantees

---

[2]Stephen R. Covey, *The 7 Habits of Highly Effective People*, page 46, Fireside, 1989.
[3]Quoted in *Speaker's Library of Business Stories, Anecdotes and Humor*, Joe Griffith, page 55.

Secrets of Personal Marketing Power

your victories. Commitment means that you give it your best. When you are totally committed to your goal you become unstoppable. To succeed, total commitment is needed.

Joe Griffith tells a story about commitment in his book *Speaker's Library of Business Stories, Anecdotes And Humor*. "Sometimes we think we are committed and we aren't. A chicken and a pig were talking about commitment. The chicken said, 'I'm committed to giving eggs every morning.' The pig said, 'Giving eggs isn't commitment, it's participation. Giving ham is total commitment.'" (page 56). The question that you have to ask of yourself is are you in participation or total commitment?

Your Personal Vision

I believe that self-assessments open doors to realizing our personal vision. It's in the process of asking questions about ourselves that we begin to look at our values, beliefs, and perceptions and how they significantly limit our personal powers. Because of our unique human capacity for self-awareness we can use self-assessments to examine our perceptions of life to determine their base of authenticity. However, we always see ourselves in our own reality. Therein lies a problem in determining a base of authenticity. Our view and perception of ourselves is largely determined by conditioning and the conditions by which we're surrounded. If our conditioning tells us that by going into business for ourselves we will only end up losing a lot of money because market conditions are bad, then we will probably not succeed and will lose our money. If our conditioning makes us believe that because we don't have a college degree we will not amount to much, chances are that it will become a self-fulfilling prophecy. However, if we acknowledge that conditioning has tremendous power in our lives but that conditioning doesn't have to control our lives, then we can change our conditions and circumstances.

In his book *The 7 Habits Of Highly Effective People*, Steven Covey talks about the habit of proactivity. He states that the habit of

Chapter 3

proactivity is the "first and most basic habit of a highly effective person in any environment," (page 71). Proactivity is simply taking the initiative in life and we are responsible for that. He states that "our behavior is a function of our decisions, not our conditions," (page 71). Highly proactive people recognize their responsibility and "they do not blame circumstances, conditions, or conditioning for their behavior," (page 71). "Their behavior is a product of their own conscious choice, based on values, rather than a product of their conditions," (page 71).

When you give yourself the freedom to choose, you free yourself of self-imposed limitations. You now take responsibility for developing your "Personal Marketing Power", and engage that power to position yourself and move more aggressively in your business. Your imagination starts to open up new innovative ideas, possibilities, visions and opportunities to employ in the self-promotion process.

When I personally had the courage to make the commitment to become a professional speaker, I began to engage the help of others and use my "Personal Marketing Power." At the time, I hadn't recognized it as power. I knew that marketing was essential to my success. I coined the phrase "Personal Marketing Power" several years ago when I was co-authoring my first book. It was then that I realized that nothing moves in mass volume to the consumer, and no one gets elected to office or moves up the corporate ladder without first developing and activating "Personal Marketing Power." Today we see CEO's and presidents of corporations taking a more active role in marketing. Lee Iacocca was responsible for the turnaround and success of the Chrysler Corporation. He was a master at marketing himself to the public. He employed some very simple marketing tools and strategies to personally promote himself to the public. Once he had gained the trust and confidence of the automobile buying public, he knew they would begin to support him by buying Chrysler products.

My goal throughout the rest of this book is to give you the tools, weapons and strategies to inspire you to develop your "Personal Marketing Power." The financial benefit, reward and satisfaction that comes from "Personal Marketing Power" are staggering. You can:

Secrets of Personal Marketing Power

- Improve and increase your personal productivity.
- Produce major results with ease and efficiency.
- Accomplish your goals through the power of others.
- Connect with people who will help in promoting you, your product, service, or idea.
- Increase your chances for opportunities.
- Create greater results in less time through making wise use of resources.
- Increase your ability to reach far beyond your own resources.
- Increase your ability to help others through information exchange.

Choosing "Personal Marketing Power"

When you have chosen "Personal Marketing Power" as your goal you empower yourself and others to accomplish great things. We haven't the luxury of resting on our laurels thinking that we, our products or services are in great demand throughout the universe. Taking care of our careers and businesses in a world of intense competition, restructuring, and corporate "rightsizing" requires us to be resourceful, proactive, creative, innovative and personal-marketing-driven to be successful.

However, be aware of some of life's biggest traps when setting up a plan for marketing yourself.

Set your goals but have the wisdom to know when tunnel vision has set in. Stay focused on the main highway of your goal, but know how to use the offramps of opportunity that might have passed you had you not kept your keen sense of awareness.

Chapter 3

> Al Ries & Jack Trout, authors of *Marketing Warfare and Horse Sense—How To Pull Ahead On The Business Track* make reference to the fact that "when you set a goal for yourself, you also put on 'blinders.'" Your miss opportunities which are not "in the main Sequence." If you know where you're going, then you are not going to see the side road which often leads to the opportunity of a lifetime. You suffer from "tunnel vision." "If there is one common mistake in marketing yourself, it is setting a personal goal and then failing to see other possibilities as they develop."[4]

> "Sometimes we stare so long at a door that is closing that we see too late the one that is open." *Alexander Graham Bell*

> "Marketing can be a positive, exciting, ethical part of your business; you do not have to become a huckster to be a good marketer." *Anthony O. Putman*

---

[4]Al Ries & Jack Trout, *Horse Sense*, page 7-8, Plume, 1992.

Part Two
THE POWER OF
NETWORKING

CHAPTER 4   Your Center of Power

CHAPTER

4

YOUR CENTER OF POWER

Personal Marketing Secret #1

"HOW NETWORKING DRIVES THE CENTER OF YOUR POWER."

Secrets of Personal Marketing Power

The center of your power is people pushing and pulling you towards your goals. When you influence and mobilize others to support you and rally around your cause you have simply exercised personal power and the synergy of people.

Networking is one of the most cost-effective and productive "Personal Marketing Power" tools we have available to us. Literally, networking drives the center of your power. However, "Personal Marketing Power" goes beyond networking.

Networking is a tactic and tool of your "Personal Marketing Power." Perhaps the best way to describe "Networking" is that it's the process of putting people in touch with other people with the idea of gathering and sharing information for mutual benefit and profiting from that relationship.

Networking is defined by Susan RoAne in her book *The Secrets of Savvy Networking*. She states that "Networking is a reciprocal process, an exchange of ideas, leads and suggestions that supports both our professional and our personal lives. There is also a spirit of sharing that transcends the information shared. The best networkers reflect that spirit with a genuine joy in their giving."[1]

Networking is nothing new. However, how we network has changed and will continue to change with the advancement of technology. The traditional form of networking has been through organizations such as social clubs, lead clubs, associations, sport clubs and political clubs—with more of a social attitude than that of an aggressive business attitude of provocation—for the collecting and dissemination of information.

Technology is changing the ways we network. We network through our computers using programs such as Compuserve, Prodigy, America Online, Video Mail, E-MAIL, Desktop Video Communications, and that's just the beginning.

> "We cannot create a positive presence unless we are present. We can stay in touch by letter, phone, fax or E-mail, but a face-to-face conversation establishes rapport like no other interaction or communication."   *Susan RoAne*[2]

---

[1]Susan RoAne, *The Secrets of Savvy Networking*, page 6, Warner Books, 1993.
[2]Susan RoAne, *The Secrets of Savvy Networking*, page 38, Warner Books, 1993.

Chapter 4

Networking has taken on a real attitude as to how we approach and couple business and social activities. Networking is a skill and the secret to successful networking is not in what you do but how effective you are in connecting with others. Your approach to successful networking requires specific skills and tools. It's those skills and tools that we need to develop mastery over so to work wisely within our networks and have all persons benefit.

"Power Networking" Golden Rules for Personal Success

Skills most essential for developing proficient and powerful networking habits are:

- Active listening. God created man and woman with two ears and one mouth and I'm sure that it wasn't for cosmetic purposes only. However, I'm always amazed how people can flap their jaws and run off at the mouth regardless of whether or not they know what they are talking about.

> "It is better to remain quiet and be thought a fool than to speak and remove all doubt."
> *Anonymous*

Networking and communications are twins and both are designed for the transference of information. Active and skillful listening will ensure that you gather valuable and important information which will increase your value as an information resource. Being viewed as an information resource (or agent, the term I commonly use in my "Personal Marketing Power" seminars) empowers you to draw more of your fellow networkers into your center of influence. With that influence comes power, trust and credibility, thus helping you accomplish your goals.

Secrets of Personal Marketing Power

> "Most of the successful people I've known are ones who do more listening than talking. If you choose your company carefully, it's worth listening to what they have to say. You don't have to blow out the other fellow's light to let your own shine." *Bernard M. Baruch*

- Asking smart questions. Contrary to popular belief, asking questions proves you're intelligent. It's sad, but unfortunately true, that most people can't bring themselves to ask questions in seminars and social situations simply because they don't want to look foolish and be subjected to ridicule by their peers, colleagues or superiors.

Knowing how to phrase your questions can eliminate the fear of asking and help you generate a positive response. A power networker looks for and creates opportunities for asking questions. They know how to be clear and explicit about what types of questions to ask.

Smart questions are always phrased to elicit a positive response. If you're not phrasing your question for a positive response, then what you can expect is a negative response.

An example of a question that would bring about a negative response is, "I don't suppose you know anyone who I could contact about . . . ?" A close-ended question posed in that way would generally get a yes or no answer and in most situations it would be no. The smart way to ask the same question that would create a greater possibility for an open-ended response is, "Who do you know I could contact about . . . ?" "Power Networkers" who ask smart questions can assume that the other person will respond with a positive answer.

People who have made a commitment to networking for developing their "Personal Marketing Power" focus on framing their questions in a way that will give them positive results. David J. Schwartz, author of *The Magic Of Getting What You Want*, writes in his book that "Asking means calling on someone for information, expressing a request or offering something in exchange for something else. Asking is positive and to be admired."[3]

---

[3]David J. Schwartz, *The Magic of Getting What You Want*, page 181, Berkeley, 1984.

Chapter 4

Here are several ways to frame smart questions.

"Tell me, whom do you know that . . . ?"
"Whom would you recommend I contact for . . . ?"
"I am looking for . . . Tell me who you know who . . . ?"
"Whom do you recommend I contact for . . . ?"

Always be clear and explicit when asking for information.

- Power Group Presentations. Communication is the most important skill in life. The basic forms of communication are listening, reading, writing, and speaking. We communicate in other ways such as how we dress, our behavior and attitude, all of which are learned skills. However, the important communication skill to which I refer is speaking or presentation. Every time we open our mouth to speak, someone listening will make a judgment about us. That judgment will either be neutral, negative or positive. If we are to interact effectively with others and influence them, we must have command of our verbal and non-verbal presentation skills.

> According to a study by Albert Meharbian in 1967 at UCLA 55% of what people respond to and make assumptions about—takes place visually—38 % of what people respond to and make assumptions about is through the sound of communications—while only 7% of what people respond to is in the actual words used.

This means that 93% of our communication takes place in how we say it and only 7% in what we say.

Therefore, to be perceived as a professional we must conduct ourselves as professionals through not only what we say but also in our actions. It's our character, actions and image we project that inspire openness and trust in others for networking opportunities.

37

- Relationship Building. Building strong relationships begins with a solid foundation of our own character, made up of our integrity, mannerisms, quality, disposition and personality. Steven Covey, in his book, *The 7 Habits of Highly Effective People*, talks about the principle of Win/Win and how it is fundamental to success. Covey states that "The principle of Win/Win is fundamental to success in all our interactions and it embraces five interdependent dimensions of life. It begins with character and moves toward relationships, out of which flow agreements," (page 216). The other two dimensions are systems, and process.

Power networkers know that a Win/Win relationship is essential to their success in networking. Building relationships is the process and it takes patience to develop the trust necessary to feel confident about referring business to someone or having someone refer business to you.

For many people networking is a fearful undertaking because it draws out one of our most common fears—the fear of rejection. Denis Waitley wrote in his book *Seeds Of Greatness* that "there are three dominant fears, beyond the fear of death:"

"Fear of Rejection, which is being made a fool or failure in the sight or presence of others."
"Fear of Change, which is charting unknown waters, being first, breaking tradition, sacrificing external security."
"Fear of Success, which is an expression of guilt associated with our natural desire for self-gratification."[4]

The interesting thing about people is that few truly want isolation or to be alone. Almost everyone needs to interact with other people. Many are eager to meet and bring new people into their lives, whether it's for intimacy, friendship or just for a brief moment. It's in reaching out for intimacy, friendship or that brief moment that we have to go beyond our fear of rejection and that takes courage.

Leonard Zunin said that "courage is seeing your fear in a realistic perspective, defining it, considering alternatives and choosing to function in spite of risk."[5]

---

[4]Denis Waitley, *Seeds Of Greatness*, page 29, Revell, 1983.
[5]Leonard Zunin, *Contact: The First Four Minutes*, page 57, Ballantine, 1973.

Chapter 4

The benefits associated with networking outweigh the false assumptions and misconceptions we have about what networking is all about. When you discover that the true essence of networking is about becoming a resource of information that is to be shared with others as opposed to just someone who is manipulative and self-serving, you'll realize that there is no foundation for fear of rejection.

- Personal Visibility. Develop a personal visibility networking plan. You must show up and be up with a positive presence as a course of action in creating personal visibility.

Susan RoAne said: "We cannot create positive presence unless we are present. We can stay in touch by letter, phone, fax, or E-mail, but a face-to-face conversation establishes rapport like no other interaction or communication."[6]

Even though we can accomplish a great deal of networking through technology, we're not ready for it to replace the all important human bonding of one-on-one meetings. Don't bungle those opportunities that networking can bring to you. Don't leave your opportunities up to chance happenings. Developing a successful personal visibility networking plan requires a well-thought-out strategy for what it is you want to accomplish.

In laying out your personal visibility networking strategy decide:

- What can networking help you accomplish?

Are you a Loan Broker, Insurance Agent, Chiropractor, Professional Speaker, Graphics Designer; a small retail business owner, sales representative in multi-level marketing, or whatever? Analyze what percentage of your business now comes from referrals. Referrals come from the current power sources in your existing network, which are customers, friends, clients, business associates, centers of influence, sponsors and the grapevine. How much time and effort have you put into cultivating these referrals? Are you getting enough referral business? If not, then how much more do you want?

---

[6]Susan RoAne, *The Secrets of Savvy Networking*, page 38, Warner Books, 1993.

Secrets of Personal Marketing Power

- In what associations, civic organizations and clubs can you be most effective?

Before you go jumping into every association, civic organization and club in your industry or community, first find out in which ones you can best serve their interest as well as your own. As a joiner you serve your interest best, and that of the association, by being an active member and participant and not just a dues-payer. A position on the board or as a member of a committee is how you can maximize your membership, personal visibility, and professional presence.

- Develop a personal visibility networking scorecard—a questionnaire to rate your performance and motivate you to stay on track. For example:

"Did I put a plan in motion to meet new people today?" Power Networkers believe other people are their greatest resource.
"Did I follow-up with the request of others in providing referrals or resources?"
"Did I introduce people to others either by sending them a note or through a personal introduction?"
"Did I attend a business function and civic event or an association meeting today?"
"If so did I display my professional presence and make myself visible to the entire group?"
"Did I participate at any event by serving as a greeter, or taking part in the program?"
"Did I hand out brochures or sample products; pass out or receive any business cards at any of the events I attended?"

At the end of every day did you send out your THANK YOU notes and handwritten letters? Also, did you look for appropriate and creative ways to express appreciation to people who helped you?

- Mastering networking protocol. Let's start with reciprocity. Susan RoAne defines reciprocity as "the cornerstone of networking. It is a common courtesy, the give-and-take

40

Chapter 4

that is the glue that makes things stick together. Giving without expectation may work in some instances. Not giving back does not."[7]

Some people are takers in life. They are the bloodsuckers and unsavory people I call the polluters of life. They will use tactics such as intimidation, insincere praise, make false promises, and will pilfer your time for information, leads and referrals. These are the people who never acknowledge you with a thank you or reciprocate in any way, shape, or form. Reciprocity should be like a fresh running stream of water circulating and flowing through your network, adding nourishment as it travels.

The universe speaks loud and clear: "What goes around, comes around." In my "Personal Marketing Power" seminars I give out resources, such as printers, business card designers, software companies, and publications to subscribe to—all of whom graciously show their appreciation in various ways. However, that unsavory polluter can strike any of us at any time, and my time came. After recommending this person to over twelve thousand of my seminar attendees in a nine-month period, not one thank you was sent to me. I got wise and cut him and his company from my resource list. The results of his lack of the networking protocol of reciprocating will cost him thousands of dollars in referral business. What a fool!

> Business Cards. Our business card is an extension of who we are and what we do, and should represent us well. Therefore, care and consideration to the design of our business cards should focus on establishing a memorable, highly visible identity. The goal of your business card is to give people a tangible way of remembering you for future contact. One way to accomplish that goal is to have your picture on it. Remember the old Chinese proverb that a picture is worth a thousand words. Mastering "Personal Marketing Power" requires high visibility. Having your picture on your business card helps you be memorable in the minds of those who receive your card.

The five objectives we want our business card to fulfill are:

---

[7]Susan RoAne, *The Secrets of Savvy Networking*, page 52, Warner Books, 1993.

Secrets of Personal Marketing Power

1. That our business card identifies who we are and what we do—that would be our name and title.
2. The name of our company.
3. How to get in contact with us via a telephone number and fax number.
4. To be attention-getting and stand out from other cards.
5. Have our picture on the card. Pictures help people recall business or social situations, encounters and events with less difficulty.

I personally take exception to the idea that a business card has to conform to the traditional standard size of fitting into a business card file or Rolodex. My reasoning for that is that today more people are toting around lap-top computers with software that manages their business and social contacts. In today's highly competitive society we need to make use of all the creative weapons we can to be memorable and compelling in our marketing. Even if it means going outside of tradition.

Be smart and discriminate in passing out your business cards. I have seen too many unsavvy people pass out their business cards like they were handbills. Proper protocol is to establish a rapport first. Passing out your business cards indiscriminately will generally prove to be ineffective and a waste of time. The smart way to pass out business cards is when there is an obvious business or social connection that requires a follow-up action to take place.

- Notes of Appreciation. There is truly a magical power in the words "Thank You". People love to be appreciated. One of the strongest, most thoughtful and meaningful methods of saying "Thank You" and showing your appreciation is through personalized handwritten note cards. Personalized handwritten cards send a message to your business and social contacts that you care. Never be neglectful in sending out "Thank You" cards; it's a smart way to communicate with people while maintaining high visibility with them. There is a golden payoff in sending personalized handwritten notecards. I remember well an individual in one of my seminars who purchased our entire company library special of training materials, val-

Chapter 4

ued well over one thousand dollars. I sent this person a personalized handwritten "thank you" postcard (as I do with all who purchase materials). Several days later I received a testimonial letter from this same person. Once again I sent a thank you card (always handwritten). Two days later I got a handwritten letter from this person. The letter contained the names of several associates that had been referred to my seminar. Again I sent another personalized handwritten "Thank You" card. The point and message of this story is that people will continue to support you as long as they receive value, respect and appreciation from you.

- Professional Presence. Your Professional Presence goes beyond professional appearance. Honesty, integrity, courtesy and respect for others are some of the characteristic qualities that make up your professional presence. Selling and servicing your customers with integrity speaks volumes about you. People in your network want to operate within a level of trust with you when they refer someone to do business with you. Let people in your network know how they should think about you and your company. Your objective is to get people in your network to draw favorable and positive conclusions about who you are and what you do. Remember that people always make a comparison before making a decision. People want to make smart decisions and will look for knowledge, insight, experience, expertise, credibility and trust. When you recognize people confidently referring others to you as well as calling on you for advice, you'll know that you're operating with high visibility and professional presence.

- Follow-Up. If you don't follow-up on referrals immediately, you're better off chasing bats in dark caves. At least you'll gain the reputation of someone who has gone entirely off his rocker or someone who's extremely courageous and involved in some kind of scientific research project. That's certainly a wiser choice than to gain the reputation of someone who can't be relied upon to follow-

Secrets of Personal Marketing Power

up promptly. Follow-up should be approached in the same manner and with the same importance as when you schedule an appointment with someone—It has the same priority on your to-do list. That simply means that if you want to enhance your reputation as someone who is reliable, organized and responsive to taking action then include follow-up on your to-do list each day. Promptly following-up and taking action on leads, referrals and promises will send a positive message to your network. People will discover the value of being associated with you because you pursue an opportunity, not with great intentions, but with dynamic action. However, don't fall victim to your busy schedule by procrastinating, which can be fatal to success. Follow-up on all leads and referrals needs to be prioritized and timely—that means that some phone calls need to be made now and not in 48 hours. With today's highly competitive marketplace and the high speed transportation of information, even a one-hour delay can mean the difference between obtaining someone's business and making an important connection or losing it.

- Stay connected with people. Have an ongoing system of staying connected with people that you have met in school, associations, clubs, work, social events as well as old customers and clients throughout your career. Let people know how your business is doing and in which direction your career is moving. The goal is to maintain high visibility with past and current contacts. Every contact has value—some greater than others for opening up opportunities in our lives. However, we all know that hindsight is 20/20 vision, which I would bet just about everyone has experienced more than once in their lifetime. I know I have and I have also burnt a few bridges along the way. Some of us just don't learn our lessons early in life. Staying well-connected means assuring yourself a better-than-average chance of having a profitable career.

Remember, when you have effectively used networking as one of your "Personal Marketing Power" tools and weapons, you have set yourself apart from the average person. People who have

44

Chapter 4

mastered the "Secrets Of Personal Marketing Power" make things happen. They take the initiative. They seize the moment and the opportunities, and empower themselves through the power and synergy of people.

Part Three
POWERS THAT INFLUENCE

CHAPTER 5   The Magic Powers of
                 Influence

CHAPTER 6   More Secret Weapons of
                 "Personal Marketing Power"

CHAPTER 7   Power Weapons that
                 Position You as an Expert

CHAPTER

5

THE MAGIC POWERS OF INFLUENCE

One of the more frequently asked questions I hear from people is, "How do I develop the magical power to influence others?" Certainly there is no magic formula, but there are some powerful weapons and tools and certain principles that create the magic that influence others. It's in our strategy and how we employ the tactics, weapons and tools, and principles that give us the power. However, don't be naive in thinking that tools alone will sustain your power or your career. One of my favorite sayings is "Power is gained with flair. But it is sustained with knowledge, care and more flair." One of the real magic powers of influence comes from being so good at what you do that you stand out above your colleagues; so good that you have been recognized as an expert in your field; so good that people will rally to your support with an overwhelming enthusiasm just for the association they would have with you or your organization.

There has been much research on the subject of principles of influence by social psychologists, primarily through observation and experimental studies in laboratories. Some of the most powerful, more frequently used psychological principles of influence are: authority, scarcity, liking, reciprocity and social proof. It's with these principles of influence that you develop your "Per-

---

49

sonal Marketing Power." It's these principles of influence that are at the core of the tactic and weapons and tools, helping you master personal marketing with high visibility and professional presence. We have all been subjected to so many of the principles for so long that rarely do we consciously perceive their power. Often we overlook their basic simplicity as a valuable marketing weapon or tool that can have a tremendous ability to direct human action. It's not my intention in this book to examine each principle's enormous force and ability to produce a distinct kind of automatic, mindless modification in our thinking and behavior so we say "yes" without thinking. However, it is my intention to deliver to you the weapons and tools in which these principles of influence are embodied. Let me give you one example of what I'm talking about by telling how the principle of scarcity was used on me. One Christmas I had found a very special and unique gift that I wanted to give a friend. As she was ringing up the sale, the clerk mentioned that she only had one more of this item left in the store and when that one sold it would deplete their entire stock for the rest of the year. After making that statement she then suggested that if I liked the gift that much I should buy the second one for another friend. If I wasn't able to find another gift as unique as the one I had just purchased, the remaining one might not be available in several days. Therefore, I thought that the best thing to do was to purchase the item for a second gift. Later, I thought to myself that the principle of scarcity influenced and played an automatic role in my decision to purchase the second gift. The principles of influence have a powerful impact in our decisions and how we operate within our lives.

> As the Chinese proverb says so eloquently:
> "The fish sees the bait, not the hook."

CHAPTER

6

MORE SECRET WEAPONS OF "PERSONAL MARKETING POWER"

The power in each one of the secrets we use for developing our personal marketing will embody one or several of the influencing principles. Just as magicians or illusionists lure their audience with their props, we seduce the marketplace with an assortment of contrivances and marketing weapons. Think of your personal marketing weapons as part of your magic kit for shaping the message that promotes and elevates you to high visibility and generates an enthusiastic response to you in the marketplace. Before deciding which weapons are best to influence, motivate and capture your audience, don't lose sight of your primary goal: to sell you, your product, idea, and service. Planning is essential, however we need to know for what it is we are planning. Yogi Berra said: "If you don't know where you're going, you could wind up someplace else." Distilled from my own experience and that of others, beware of some impractical ideas to which some, too often, fall prey.

When employing marketing weapons that require copy such as newsletters, newspaper articles, and brochures—regardless if you're going for the hard-sell or the soft-sell—always use words that sell. Become a word magician or hire those that can gear your words to the needs and taste of your readers and which favorably positions you in their minds.

Secrets of Personal Marketing Power

> "The man who says it can't be done is liable to be interrupted by someone doing it." *Anonymous*

Personal Marketing Secret #2

"ACTIVATE YOUR CREATIVE POWERS TO OPEN DOORS OF OPPORTUNITY."

> "Creative people can be found in all departments in an orgainzation: data processing, engineering, sales, research and development, operations, finance, marketing, and human resources. The ability to generate original thinking has little to do with job function or even formal education."[1]

> "Call it brain power, intellectual capital, creative assets, or whatever, thinking is the new competitive weapon."[2]

The new age of consumerism has swung the doors of opportunity wide open, in regional as well as new international markets, for small and large businesses alike to grow and prosper. It's also becoming increasingly clear that with the new age of consumerism and the global economy sprouting new markets all around, we find ourselves shoulder deep in new challenges and pressures. These challenges and pressures are brought about by new technology—new technology that has become the equalizer and

---

[1]Donald W. Blohowiak, author of *Mavericks*, page 7, Irwin, 1992.
[2]Donald W. Blohowiak, author of *Mavericks*, page 8, Irwin, 1992.

Chapter 6

enabled many small businesses to be highly competitive in today's enormous marketplace. However, new technololgy alone will not be our salvation in a competitive market. With the mounting pressure competition on all sides to innovate and bring in products of greater quality with slimmer margins, we've got to begin to outsmart our competitors. The future is here. Today, we need to outsmart, outthink and outmarket the competition. The race will go to those marathoners who are the nation's stewards of innovation, creativity, and have great imaginations. The challenge is in our willingness to go outside the stereotypes—to change and be creative in the process.

> "People have the freedom to be creative, a place
> that brings out the best in everybody."
> *Jack Welch, CEO of General Electric*

CHAPTER

7

POWER WEAPONS THAT POSITION YOU AS AN EXPERT

Personal Marketing Secret #3

"MARKETING WITH NEWSLETTERS BUILDS IMAGE AND CREDIBILITY."

Personal marketing with newsletters creates a power base for you to promote yourself, your products, and services. Newsletters are ideal marketing weapons:

- Establishing yourself as an authority in your field.
- When targeted to the right customer base, newsletters give you high visibility, recognition, build an image, and maintain an all-important communication channel to increase sales.
- Newsletters have four times the readership of standard advertising.
- You enhance your credibility with newsletters.

Secrets of Personal Marketing Power

The WINNING Edge...
"Innovative Techniques & Strategies" for Developing Personal Marketing Power

Newsletter   *Volume IX*   *Spring of 1994*

For A Bright Future Speak Well In Public

Are You Prepared To Speak?

"The human brain starts working the moment you are born and never stops until you stand up to speak in public."

George Jessel

Every year baseball players go through the rigors of spring training. Getting back to basics, working on style, pitching, hitting, outfielding and perfecting their athletic abilities are vitally important for good performance. They mentally and physically condition themselves for the game to entertain and perform superbly for their fans, (audiences)---all the time learning new techniques and strategies to play the game better and better.

Speaking is not exempt from training. Like baseball players, speakers must perfect their performance skills. Working on delivery, voice quality, verbal as well as non-verbal skills are essential. Learning new innovative techniques (visual media), strategies and human technologies help us deliver a clear, persuasive and entertaining message that increases motivation and productivity in the workplace.

The best way to improve and get into shape and remain in shape is through audio/video feedback, coaching and practice. As Pat O'Malley said "Speeches are like babies, easy to conceive, hard to deliver." With video feedback and coaching we learn about our best presentation styles and see ourselves as others see us. As a result we are better positioned to set a positive climate and ensure our delivery to meet the needs of the audience.

Today, the fear of public speaking remains the #1 phobia in people. Burt Rubin of Roundhouse Square Phobia Treatment Center says "Fear of flying is probably the second-biggest phobia behind public speaking." *Both have a tremendous negative impact in the workplace* in our fast-paced global economy. Therefore, it's extremely important for all managers, sales professionals, speakers and trainers to develop fresh, eye-opening presentations and meetings that reach out and serve the needs of our audience.

P. S. Get in shape now, sign up to be in our *Spring* Workshop. (Details inside)

- Newsletters are the perfect personal marketing and targeted marketing vehicles.

Personal Marketing with newsletters is effective in any industry or profession. Loan brokers, insurance agents, lawyers, certified public accountants, real estate brokers, doctors, churches, associations, hospitals, charities, small businesses, and large corporations all use newsletters for communicating and receiving the benefit of direct sales dollars, recruitment and business development.

The frequency of circulation, size, type, design & layout of

Chapter 7

newsletters will vary. However, there are some basic fundamentals to consider in order to maximize marketing results with your newsletter. Develop your newsletter to promote specific performance goals, always keeping in mind your objective and the end result benefits. The following are some basic fundamentals and goals you want your newsletter to accomplish.

1. Develop your newsletter to invite action from your reader to:
   a. buy your products and services.
   b. attend a seminar or convention.
   c. bring in new customers.
   d. bring back old customers.
   e. win support and referrals.
   f. educate, entertain, and increase involvement.
2. Build recognition and image with your newsletter.
   a. put your picture in your newsletter.
   b. put your employees picture' in your newsletter.
   c. include your company or organization's logo in your newsletter
   d. write your mission statement in your newsletter.
   e. list your products and services in your newsletter.
   f. Print testimonials in your newsletter.
   g. reinforce your image in your newsletter with high content information, design, color and paper quality.
   h. use humor, inform and entertain your readers with cartoons, quotes and illustrations.
   i. reprint any press releases on you or quotes from articles written about you or your company.
   j. list awards and honors you have received.
3. Make it easy for your readers to respond to you. Show them what action to take and how to take it.
   a. provide a reply discount coupon for your reader.
   b. provide them with a toll-free 800 number to call you.
   c. create a self-addressed, stamped order form.
   d. include a fax-back survey & order form
4. Set performance goals to maximize results in your personal marketing.
   a. increase revenue by 15%.
   b. target new patients and increase patients by 20%.

Secrets of Personal Marketing Power

   c. upsale your products to existing seminar attendees by 25%.
   d. increase your membership by 12%.
   e. increase community use of your fitness center by 35%.

When charting out your course, develop the design and content of your newsletter, that will best serve the interests of your reader as well as meet your promotional goals, is not always simple. Staying current on consumer trends and industry information will help you develop effective visuals and valuable content. Take formal and informal surveys of your readers to find out what they want to read in your newsletter. Read trade association and industry magazines to get additional information. Your newsletter is an essential strategy in your overall personal marketing plan. So, set your promotional goals and your objectives, your strategies in place, and develop the best newsletter around.

Here is some good advice for you to follow: Publishing your newsletter will require the use of statistical information, reprint of copyright information, photographs of people, and drawings/ illustrations and cartoons. All of these will require you obtain permission to use them. Also, this advice holds true for any books or monographs you may write. Here are samples of the permission request forms that you will be required to use.

PHOTO/ILLUSTRATION RELEASE

I hereby grant to _____ the right to reproduce and publish my photograph or likeness in his book/newsletter entitled _____ to be published by _____ in any manner they may see fit.

Description of photo to be used : **ATTACHED**

Signature _____

Name _____

Address _____

City, State, Zip _____

Phone Number _____

Date _____

58

Chapter 7

I am preparing a newsletter to be published by _____ in March 1994. The book/newsletter is entitled _____ by _____ . It will have approximately _____ pages, a tentative subscription price of $ _____ , and initial print run/circulation of _____ copies. It will be published in the United States, its territories, Canada and Mexico.

May _____ have your permission to use the following material in this newsletter and in future printings and editions? These rights will in no way restrict republication of your material in any other form by you or others authorized by you. If you do not control these rights in their entirety, would you kindly let me know whom else I must contact?

Selection: _____

By: _____

From: _____

The following credit line will be used unless otherwise indicated:

_____

I would appreciate your consent to this request as soon as possible. If you have any questions regarding this request, please call me at _____ . For your convenience a release form is provided below for you to sign and a copy of this letter enclosed for your files.

Sincerely,

_____

I grant permission for the use requested above:

_____   _____
(name)   (signature)

_____   _____
(Social Security/Federal ID #)   (date)

59

Secrets of Personal Marketing Power

Personal Marketing Secret #4

"HOW TO GET YOUR CUSTOMERS TO PAY FOR YOUR MARKETING WITH AUDIO NEWSLETTERS & AUDIO MAGAZINES."

Every month I receive an audio tape from the National Speakers' Association entitled "Voices of Experience." The format basically consists of interviews with top professionals in the speaking and seminar business who discuss the way in which they have become successful in a very lucrative and competitive industry. The information and topics can range from how to work with a speaker's bureau to customizing your program for client satisfaction—all of which is very important, informative and stimulating, regardless of age and experience as a speaker. Each and every month, I look forward to receiving "Voices of Experience", and each time I listen I get valuable information, tips and techniques on how to be a better business person and speaker. The audio Newsletter/Magazine is just one marketing tool that

Chapter 7

helps the association stay connected with its members. It's a marketing strategy you can employ to stay well-connected with your customers, bring in new customers, sell more products and services and be paid a subscription fee.

Here are several formats for creating a winning audio

Newsletter/Magazine:

- The interview format. A host interviews a guest who is an authority on a particular subject.
- The newscast approach. Someone speaks directly to the listening audience, absent of any two-way dialogue.
- The panel format. Several panelists discuss a variety of subjects.
- It can be produced using a combination of several formats.

Program Ideas

- A stock broker could have an audio newsletter of the month with tips on what to look for in a particular company before buying stock in that company.
- A personal fitness trainer could have a program interviewing nutritional experts on the proper diet to maintain for better health.
- A financial planner could have a financial forum program to talk about how economic changes affect financial goals.
- A sales and marketing training company would have a program on marketing methods and sales strategies.

The ideas and opportunities for using audio Newsletters/ Magazines to personally market yourself are endless. In your programming, you can inform the listener of new products and services available from your company; events that would be of value to your customers. Blow your horn a little—have a personal message about your accomplishments (just don't over-embellish).

Make sure the following information is recorded on your audio Newsletter/Magazine so that it's ccnvenient for your customer to reach you for placement of orders or get additional information:

Secrets of Personal Marketing Power

> Your Company Name
> Your Company Address
> Your 800 number
> Your Fax number
> Let the listener know how to subscribe to your audio News-
> letter/Magazine

At the conclusion of your audio portion invite your listener to share this audio Newsletter/Magazine with a friend—better yet, tell them to copy the tape and send it to whomever they wish. A percentage of these people will become new subscribers and new customers. Remember, you are a personal marketing maverick and want as much name recognition and opportunities to bring in more business as possible.

Personal Marketing Secret #5

"GET PUBLISHED IN OTHER NEWSLETTERS."

Let your imagination soar, open up your creative channels of thinking and start listing with pen and paper in hand all the newsletters that exist in your industry. If you are unaware of your industry's newsletters, then do some research at your local library. Get on the phone to your customers, vendors, and associations and find out which newsletter they receive and/or publish themselves. Ask them to send you copies. Once you have these newsletters in your possession, browse through them, studying the information, articles and editorial format. This will give you a good idea of how to slant your article for publication in their newsletter. Also, some newsletter editors will conduct personal interviews and take excerpts from other written works such as books, articles, reports or research that you have written and had published. Write a letter to the editor or, better yet, call to get relevant article guidelines and the name and address of the proper contact person. Keep in mind that most company newslet-

Chapter 7

SERVICE...
Our commitment that never expires.

Call today: 800/ 264-9250   412/ 374-9250

March, 1994 — **The Mortgage Update**

Don Price Offers "Personal Marketing Power"

When marketing, don't focus on what your company offers your buyers and sellers, says sales trainer and author Don Price. "*Personal Marketing Power* means selling yourself," he explains.

Price adds that "if you are seen favorably in the eyes of consumers, the rest falls into place." He encourages real estate agents today to "market first, and sell second."

Positioning yourself with a good image — and then promoting that — will insure that you have a steady stream of business.

"Be bold and creative in your marketing," Price continues. "Take risks. Don't look at what your competition is doing, and you'll then develop something unique."

Marketing takes patience, he adds, and is an ongoing process. "It's an investment — not an expense," says Price.

Sales Trainer Don Price:
"Marketing is an investment — not an expense."

GOOD INVESTMENTS
"Tell your customers why they are smart to be working with you," he adds. Price favors using these marketing tools to get your message across:

✔ *Testimonial letters* let a happy customer speak on your behalf. Your customers are most apt to believe what someone else says about you.

✔ *Photo business cards* help make you memorable. Price explains that 80 percent of all business cards are thrown out within 30 minutes of being given to someone. But photo cards are more likely to be kept.

✔ *Newsletters and brochures* sell for you when you can't be in someone's home or office. Traditional printed ones — as well as audio and video formats — all can be used successfully.

✔ *Seminars* allow you to present yourself before a group of good prospects.

continued on page two

In This Issue:
- Good News — Rates Edge Up
- Lowest Fixed Rates
- Making 1994 More Successful
- Great Time to Buy!

What to Expect from a Loan Officer

Offering competitive rates every day is part of our services as mortgage loan officers. But good rates by themselves do not insure that your buyer's needs will be met.

Here are three questions you should ask a loan officer before trusting him or her with one of your transactions:

1 *Will you understand the needs of my customers?*
We begin by listening. And then we ask questions to find out about your customers.
If they are to be truly happy homeowners for years — the kind who will call on you again when they are ready to move up to a

continued on page two

Success Guide for Real Estate Professionals

Sample Newsletter—The Mortgage Update,
Copyright © 1994, publisher Howard Schneider.

ters don't have a huge network of staff like a magazine or newspaper. Typically, the staff may consist of one person, which could be the president of the company, the president's administrative assistant or—more than likely—it could be published under the direction of the human resource department. The wizardry of personal marketing through others' newsletters comes from your ability to think of as many opportunities as possible, and all the imaginable ways, you can get in print. The next step is to be prepared when the opportunity presents itself.

Secrets of Personal Marketing Power

About Opportunity.

Opportunity is all around us every nanosecond of our day, ceaselessly presenting itself squarely in our face—but seldom do we recognize it. My father always used to talk about how one has to always be aware when opportunity is staring you in the face, but most importantly he said one has to be prepared for it when it presents itself. A young man and woman just out of college wanted to know the secret of fame, fortune and success. They approached a very wealthy and successful elderly gentleman and asked what his great secret to fame, fortune and success was. The elderly gentlemen's reply was that "There is no secret, except—jump to the opportunity when it presents itself." The young man and woman, somewhat puzzled, asked, "How can we tell when opportunity is present?" "You can't," replied the elderly gentleman, "you just have to keep jumping."

> Charles Schwab, the legendary president of Bethlehem Steel, once explained to a reporter that, "All of us are products of circumstance or opportunity. The trouble is that a lot of us don't see our opportunities soon enough—or don't use them in the right way. I simply did the best I could with the chances I got. He who does his best, does all that he can. He who does less than his best, does nothing."

Here are several smart ideas that you can use to seek out your opportunity to be published in others' newsletters:

- I ask the people who attend my seminars if their company has a newsletter that is published monthly. If so, I let them know that I would be more than willing to contribute an article or be interviewed for their next edition. I have innumerable requests—I believe I've opened a Pandora's Box.
- Are you a personal fitness trainer? Let your corporate clients know that you would write an article for their

Chapter 7

newsletter. You could title it "Ten Exercise Tips For Peak Performance."

- Are you a CPA & financial planner? If so, find those newsletters that target your market and submit an article such as "How To Audit-Proof Yourself From The IRS."
- Are you a investment counselor, with clients connected with several large corporations? If so, write an article in their newsletter. If there are some heavy stock buyers you could title it: "Ten Reasons For Selling A Stock."

To have a successful personal marketing campaign, you can't be perfectly content with writing just one article merely to gain public attention once. A savvy personal marketer creates a tidal wave of optimal exposure. Just how many newsletters, and how many times do you have to be in print? As much and as many times as will favorably position you to maximize your business growth.

Personal Marketing Secret #6

"BUILD AND PUMP-UP YOUR CAREER WITH NEWS ARTICLES."

News Articles can be your most effective marketing tool, personal and persuasive like a one-on-one sales presentation. Articles written for magazines and trade journals are your one personal marketing power tool that will pump-up and help establish your credibility as an authority, edify your message, and promote your products and services.

Warning—the one time article has little, if any, value. As a savvy personal marketing maverick, you'll need to know a plain and crucial fact—one article is not enough to underscore your professional presence in the marketplace. To make your mark and be perceived and acknowledged as an expert and indispensable, you will want to resign your thinking to mass production. You can often write the same article several different ways simply by

Secrets of Personal Marketing Power

rearranging and changing the content of your material to fit each publication.

Crucial to quickly shimmying up the pole to celebrity status in your targeted industry is to have multiple articles simultaneously in several of that industry's publications. Another tactic is to have a series of articles published in one magazine. A colleague of mine had seven monthly articles published because the editor liked the topic and the message of his articles. This helped him get established in a new industry for speaking engagements and seminars. Stay focused on your objective. Writing articles is for the purpose of personally marketing yourself and it is a lure to hook in new prospective clients and customers. Don't expect to be paid in money for your articles. Your payment will come in other ways:

- Increased visibility & recognition.
- Inquiries for your products and services.
- Paid consulting fees.
- Paid speaking engagements.
- Radio and TV appearances.

The savoir-faire of personal marketing is to be media-worthy, thus getting maximum media exposure for yourself.

Begin by finding local trade journals and magazines or specific company publications. To find these, go to your library for some assistance. There are directories that will help you locate the right sources for you. You presumably subscribe to several magazines that would be worth pursuing. There are literally hundreds of publications in every field. Select those that would be of interest to you, call the editor, and ask for information on how to submit your article to their publication. The editor may send you a media submission package outlining copyright information, length of article, to be sent on hard copy or computer disk etc. Always inquire about having your picture published with your article. Also, grant only first-time publication rights for your article so that you can use articles later for other promotional products. Granting first-time only publication rights lets you retain ownership of your materials without having to get permission to rework the article for your own use.

Here are a few simple rules to follow:

Chapter 7

- Send your article as requested—right length and story slant.
- Once accepted, send your article in promptly.
- Send your biographical information.
- Send a good quality black & white photograph of yourself (8" x 10" or 5" x 7").
- Request copies of the printed publication for your marketing kit.

The Secret is Out—Getting Writers to Write about You

For the professional writer to have a high profile and successful writing career, that person must first have something to write about. From the interviews I've had with professional writers, they tell me that their number one objective is to find a story that sells. The writer's business is looking for interesting people and topics to write about. You have to make it your business to be interesting enough for the writer to do a feature story on you.

I frequently get featured in magazines and national newsletters such as *The Mortgage Update* published by *The Mortgage Times* for mortgage bankers and brokerage firms across the nation. I had been following their feature stories for more than six months. Sales trainers Tom Hopkins, Tony Alessandra, Barb Schwarz and Floyd Wickman were just a few who were all featured in a lead article, each in a different month. It never occurred to me or the editor of *The Mortgage Update* that I would make for an excellent lead article in this newsletter. The reason it never occurred to the editor was that I was marketing heavily into the mortgage industry and the newsletter was targeted at real estate agents. The editor had done several feature articles on me in magazines for the mortgage industry. I called him and suggested that I be featured in the next issue and reminded him that Personal Marketing applies to all industries and all professions. He agreed. The point is that you not have blinders on or have myopic vision when it comes to watching out for writers who potentially would jump to write a story about your topic.

Here's how to go about finding a writer:

Secrets of Personal Marketing Power

- Select magazines, newspapers, newsletters and industry journals that would give you the greatest promotional value.
- Watch for stories and interviews that are similar to yours. For example, the article that appeared in the first chapter of this book, written by Curtis Ingham and entitled "Playing For Keeps", may be a mirror of your story. If so, call Curtis Ingham and explain to him that you have a interesting story that he may want to write about.

Whenever you appear as a speaker, or at a book signing at a local book store, or a charity fund raiser, don't keep it a secret— let the print media in on the program.

Chapter 7

Use Seminars to Obtain Bookings, Consulting, and Product Sales

by Don L. Price, CA

If you do not market and sell your products, consulting, and program bookings through public seminars, you may be losing out on an extremely cost effective way to:
1. Increase your client base.
2. Triple product sales.
3. Build an effective lead generating system.

Seminars are an alternative to cold calls, direct mail, or other kinds of advertising. Many companies use seminars to market and sell products and services. Waddell & Reed, Inc. and law firms that offer living trust seminars, computer firms, real estate seminar promoters, insurance companies, and other financial firms offer free seminars at great expense. The only way they can recoup their promotional cost is to factor expenses back in by the number of sales made at the free seminars.

Our services do not have a broad mass market appeal, so we have created a highly successful and different approach to obtaining new consulting and speaking contracts, and product sales. We work on the premise that marketing our services through seminars creates a high-quality lead generating system to obtain new clients, and our seminars are also a profit center. To accomplish this, we set:

Three major objectives
1st: Offer profitable selling seminars with high content material for which we charge a fee.
2nd: Sell high-end education materials at the seminar.
3rd: Convert our seminar attendees into clients as an after-sale to the seminar, and sell our educational materials.

To accomplish these goals successfully and with regular frequency requires a flexible system, an experimental approach to advertising, and target markets.

Five Key Ideas
a. We promote heavily in newspapers. Copy and placement of our ads are more critical than size. (Big is not always better.)
b. Frequency in major metropolitan cities is 90 days to produce maximum attendance. Fewer days literally cuts attendance to less than half. Over 90 days bears no significant increase.
c. Location of hotels where we stage seminars has a serious impact on a large or small turnout. (In New York commuters use subways. Downtown Manhattan draws a larger group than a venue at Kennedy or La Guardia Airports.
d. Selling a high price set of educational manuals at our seminars dramatically increases dollar profits and volume, and gives better pre-qualified leads for additional bookings and consulting contracts.
e. Powerful and persuasive group-selling skills with high educational content; adding a flavor of humor, caring, compassion, and lots of enthusiasm is paramount to making seminars work effectively.

Use Seminars to Obtain Bookings, Consulting, and Product Sales, page 20. Copyright © 1991, Sharing Ideas News Magazine, (818) 335-8069.

Secrets of Personal Marketing Power

Position Yourself in the Marketplace

by Don Price

No matter what the market conditions are, loan agents need to position themselves in the marketplace to maintain a high level of production. To do so requires having a plan of action that is innovative and creative for having an ongoing flow of quality leads and referrals.

However, most originators make bad decisions on how to develop a market presence and position themselves in the marketplace. By positioning, I mean creating an innovative and tactical campaign that defines your role in the marketplace, as an expert and the best in the industry.

For instance, some originators prefer using alternative documentation and thus specialize in fast funding. Quick turnaround is their position. However, in today's marketplace, fast funding and quick turnaround is not good enough. Borrowers need to know specifically why it's smart to do business with you.

Whatever marketing tools you use should then get that message across—and the role of marketing is to deliver those messages with a highly creative approach to be distinctive and compelling.

All this sounds obvious, thus most loan originators use the same old "me too" marketing slogans as everyone else:
- "We have lots of programs to choose from."
- "We offer great service."
- "Call us for the lowest rates."

By being that general and trying to appeal to a broad, mass audience, many originators come across as just another loan agent in the industry. Few will remember their messages. Why does this happen? Most originators have not been trained or more often, don't understand what and how important marketing is.

In today's highly competitive and creative marketplace, we must choose our marketing carefully, and have it be very targeted. Let me give you my definition of marketing—broken down into two stages.

The first stage: Marketing is the process that favorably positions your company, product or service in the mind of the customer.

The second stage: Personal marketing is the process that favorably positions you in the mind of the customer.

One of our most cost-effective marketing strategies is developing a strong referral base of satisfied customers who spread the word to friends and family members. Nothing could be more targeted than that. And, it will happen faster if you have what I call "Personal Marketing Power". With this quality you will stand out, rather than appear to be just another loan originator.

Your "Personal Marketing Power" is developed by mobilizing all your mental and physical resources to effectively self promote and position yourself favorably in the marketplace. The traditional "good rates-good service-good loan selection" trilogy which most originators rely on, has little affect today. "Personal Marketing Power" means that you will develop a unique approach to telling others what you do.

> Be so compelling in your marketing that your prospects and customers will remember you as a person on whom they could rely to get things done.

We need to market boldly and creatively. Again, it's important to be very specific in order to position yourself. Although you might offer dozens of loan types, your target audience will remember you best if they see you as an expert in one area.

Instead of telling about how many lenders have approved you, position yourself as a person who gets results in your loan specialty. Be so compelling in your marketing that your prospects and customers will remember you as a person on whom they could rely to get things done.

Chapter 7

INSIDE BUSINESS

By Jackie Howe

DON L. PRICE - Dynamic Professional Speaker And Seminar Leader

How does a man who believes in the power of American business act on that belief?

One dynamic entrepreneur does it by bringing commitment and enthusiasm to his profession as a professional speaker and by sharing his skills and insights through seminars on persuasion, negotiation and communication.

Don L. Price shows those in his seminars step-by-step methods on how to increase their power through effective communication and persuasion skills to influence others.

Through the use of newly developed human technologies, Price Seminars help individuals to:

• Increase understanding and productivity among employees and customers;

• Develop a cooperative environment necessary for utilizing the basic skills and techniques essential for successful negotiations;

• Effective sales presentations - power speaking before one or one-thousand;

• Build better and stronger relationships, both in one's personal and business life.

He compares these skills to tools, which can be used over and over to enable a person to reach his goals.

As he talks, Price displays enthusiasm for what he does, both through his attitude and his environment. He sits on the edge of his chair as he describes both his particular style of serving clients and of starting others on new pathways of success in their endeavors. He is surrounded by his collection of books and magazines about business, selling, and personal improvement.

"One of my greatest interests is the area of personal development," Price said. "I'm always interested in ways people do things. Even when I travel, I like to experience the culture of the area to see what motivates the people - what turns them on to life."

He said that although he has always been intrigued by how people do things in general, he became interested in personal development during a hospital stay when he read "I'm OK, You're OK." Since then, he has been challenging himself to add energy and excitement to every area of his life.

"I have read more than 350 books, from almanacs to art to how-to's, and *I have found, universally, that things usually gravitate to 'basics.'*"

He said that many people interpret this to mean we should avoid progress. Price disagrees, saying that it means we must simply simplify the process.

In his work, he simplifies the complicated world of business and selling with the concept of "service" while concentrating on his commitment to serving the needs of clients and customers.

> *"Even when I travel, I like to experience the culture of the area to see what motivates people - what turns them on to life."*

Secrets of Personal Marketing Power

Personal Marketing Secret #7

*"BE A SELF-PROMOTION
PERSONAL MARKETING
MAVERICK—RADIO INTERVIEWS
POSITION YOU AS AN EXPERT
IN YOUR FIELD."*

The first time I was called by a producer to be interviewed on radio I went into a state of consternation. I thought to myself that there was absolutely no way that I was going to get though this interview without tripping all over my tongue. However, there is a bigger challenge ahead of you than worrying about tripping over your tongue. For you to succeed as a personal marketing maverick you need to create a media action plan. The media may seem complex at times, so carefully review each radio station in your marketing area as to how they differ from one another. Learn the differences and understand what kinds of guests the stations feature. Knowing the listening audience profile will help you determine if it's the right station for meeting your goals and objectives. Two ways to gather this information is to contact people whom you know have had experience with being interviewed on radio talk shows. The other is to go through published sources at your library, such as Nielsen Media Research, Sales and Marketing Research and MediaMark Research; or hire a media relations consultant who will identify the right stations for you in your marketing area. Once you have targeted the stations that best fit your overall marketing objectives, you'll need to package yourself and your product or service so the station recognizes that you're the perfect guest. If you have written a book, produced an educational video series or audio tape series, created a new invention, made a discovery, developed a new product, are controversial, or a social activist, then you need to be on radio. Talk radio can be right for almost any individual, business, organization, association or group. Talk radio may not make you

Chapter 7

a star, but certainly a leading authority in your field. Your success on radio will come from how compelling, knowledgeable and authoritative your are. Your listening audience will expect from you ideas that are capable of improving their lives, inspiring new hope and solving problems.

They want you to be the master of purveying hope.

Selling Your Topic to the Media

Prepare your selling message before contacting a radio station. You have to prepare a clear sales message as to why their audience should be interested in you. Show the producer of the show how you and your subject can help assist in meeting their programming objectives. Have support materials covering your topic prepared and available. Present yourself with a professional flair. Demonstrate that you're dependable and can deliver what you promise.

The Introduction

Never leave the importance of your introduction to a chance happening. A well-written introduction will set the tone and pace of your interview. Write your introduction to position yourself as an expert worthy of notice. A forty-five to sixty word introduction of yourself that presents you in the best light is an appropriate length.

I personally believe an introduction should present you with a flair that will reach-out and grab the attention of the listeners. Traditionally, an introduction should include:

- your name.
- your title and company.
- any relevant degrees you hold.
- books you have written.
- any relevant awards you have received.
- any magazine or newspaper article about you.

Here is an example of one of my introductions:

73

Secrets of Personal Marketing Power

> "Don Price, president of Don L. Price & Associates, Redondo Beach, California, is a dynamic and inspiring nationally recognized speaker and author of the best-selling book *Secrets Of Personal Marketing Power—Strategies For Achieving Greater Personal & Business Success*. Don will share his unparalleled innovative strategies and insights on how to market masterfully and be financially independent."

Preparation is the key to having a successful interview on radio. Complete an outline on your subject to include any statistics, people involved, geographic area, the importance and benefits of your subject, etc. Also, write a complete list of questions for your radio talk show host. Help the host conduct a good interview. You're the expert on your subject and a list of good clear questions will help bring out the most important features and give your host a track to run on. If you have written a book, appeared on another radio or TV program, or have appeared in print, send a copy of your book, tapes of other interviews, and copies of articles to the host.

Media tips for a promising and successful promotion:

- Timing is the key. If your topic is hot, you're on—if not, ask to be kept on file.
- Don't embellish or over-hype your story.
- Present yourself professionally by being prepared.
- When selling to the media make your points cut to the chase and be considerate of their time.
- Sell the guts of the story—develop the hook or slant that sells.
- Study the station first. Is there a good fit?
- If you are creating a media blitz be available and flexible.
- Don't present yourself as a huckster. Avoid repeating the name of your book, product or event throughout the interview.
- NEVER, NEVER say anything you don't want broadcasted.

Chapter 7

Personal Marketing Secret #8

"THINK INNOVATIVELY ABOUT TV TALK SHOWS."

> "The people who get on in this world are the ones who get up and look for the circumstances they want, and if they can't find them, make them."   *George Bernard Shaw*

A bright future, fame and fortune requires creative vision and a good personal marketing plan that gets you tons of free publicity. If you're going to be successful in maximizing your personal marketing, then you'll want to include the talk show programs in your personal marketing public relations campaign. In addition to talk shows, there are numerous educational programs that may be worthy of your pursuit. Be aware, however, that TV as we know it today is making major changes in format and the number of channels that will be available for future opportunities. Smart personal marketing requires re-thinking our strategy for getting free publicity in the electronic media. As it becomes more interactive with many channels TV will offer a narrowed and targeted format that will allow us to reach our selected market quickly.

Your success with getting on the TV talk circuit will be largely determined by your skill at selling yourself and how well you have organized your media campaign. If you haven't got the experience or right contacts for implementing a media campaign, you may consider hiring a public relations consultant to work with you.

Secrets of Personal Marketing Power

Personal Marketing Secret #9

"POWER-UP YOUR CAREER BY WRITING YOUR FIRST BOOK."

We live in an increasingly complex society. A society that is rife with violent crime, obesity, drugs, alcohol, hopelessness, acts of child abuse and molestation, sex crimes, fraud and embezzlement. It all sounds pretty grim, doesn't it? However, there is a positive side to all of this insane and senseless behavior. You may be an expert in the field of drug and alcohol rehabilitation, an expert on violent crime, a personal fitness trainer, or perhaps you're tops in your field of sales & marketing. If so, write a book. Also, yours may be one of the millions of human interest stories such as someone who fought hard to overcome cancer and, against great odds, survived to tell the story. People all around us are looking for the answers to solving their problems. The problems can range from how to be a better husband or better wife, to how to start a home-based business, to how to reshape your figure, and to how to sell more in less time. If you're an expert in child psychology, at writing newsletters, in negotiating, networking, or an expert in real estate and want to excel and build your business, then write a book. A book positions you as an expert in your field. Your value will increase substantially. It's the one Personal Marketing Weapon that will be the key to unlock the doors to guest appearances on network shows, radio and speaking engagements.

Writing and having your book published can be financially rewarding. Every time you appear as a guest speaker, conduct a seminar, are interviewed on talk radio or appear as a guest on a network show, expect to sell a ton of your books. If you become a best-selling author like such celebrities as Harvey MacKay, Faith Popcorn, Dr. Wayne W. Dyer, Anthony Robbins, Danielle Kennedy, Stephen R. Covey—watch out. There's no telling what lucky breaks will come your way.

Chapter 7

Your Road to Having
Your Book Published

The first step is to write your book. When you have completed the writing, submit your manuscript to a publisher. Many times this involves a long difficult process which may involve a literary agent working with you to find a publisher willing to publish your book.

In the resource section I've listed my recommendations for more information on how to become a published author.

A second option is to self-publish your book. The first business book I co-authored was self-published. There are a countless number of ways to self-publish your book. Many authors take the low-budget approach for their first book. The author simply writes on a word processor or uses desktop publishing software. With the excellent software programs on the market today, it is increasingly difficult to detect the difference between a professional publishing company's product and that of a self-publisher's. Low-budget books are printed in an 8 1/2" x 11" format, three-hole punched and then placed in a three ring binder, or they are comp-bound, wire-bound or, in some rare situations, they may be perfect-bound.

The second format for your self-published book is in hard-back or soft-back cover, perfect bound. The size will range from less than 5" x 7" to 8 1/2" x 11" with an average size of 6" x 9".

If you choose self-publishing, I have listed several excellent resources in the resource section of this book which should prove helpful.

You may not be ready to take on the monumental task and challenge of writing a book at this very moment in your life, but you have some information that is valuable and others are more than willing to pay for it. There are several things to consider:

- First, if all the materials and research you have for your book are in some disarray and that's holding you back, or you have concerns about your writing ability, stop right there. Those are not legitimate reasons or excuses for avoiding writing your book. There are writers who do

77

Secrets of Personal Marketing Power

nothing but write books for people like yourself. They are skilled and experienced in assembling your materials, researching information, and helping with the cover design, printing and marketing.

- Second, write a monograph, which is simply a mini-report of your information.

O.K., so you don't have enough material to fill the pages of a book consisting of two hundred and six pages, however, your valuable, hard-to-locate information will fill twenty to forty pages. Great!

Remember, it's information for helping people solve their problems that you're selling, not thick stacks of irrelevant paper glued at one end with a nice glossy cover. However, don't let me confuse you about nice glossy covers. To position your information in the marketplace takes creative and innovative marketing and the nice glossy cover with the right words printed on it may represent the difference between success and failure. Writing a monograph will provide you with authorship credibility. It will further your image, enhance your professional presence and reputation, and ultimately increase your value in the marketplace.

Personal Marketing Secret #10

"HOW TEACHING AN ADULT EDUCATION CLASS IS OFTEN OVERLOOKED AS A SMART PERSONAL MARKETING CONCEPT."

Smart marketers are using every strategy, concept, idea, and methodology to out-market their competition. Smart marketers look for ways to engineer and design their marketing to reach financially rewarding levels of high sales with high profits. Teaching an adult education course is another very favorable way to

Chapter 7

build a strong lead generation system, a strong prospecting list for consulting assignments, and to get additional exposure in your market area as an expert in the field. Hundreds of opportunities are available for you to take advantage of personally marketing though teaching others what you do. If you haven't thought of the wide range of adult classes given every night across this county as a very profitable marketing tool, you might want to reconsider your thinking. You can find people from all professions marketing their services and products. Dr. David Viscott, the famous psychotherapist, author Nathaniel Branden, Dan Poynter, the self-published author of more than sixty books, Dr. M. Scott Peck, Dr. Bernie Siegel, world renowned expert on health and healing, and Dr. Wayne Dyer, author of *Your Erroneous Zones* and *Real Magic*, are just a few of those who have marketed themselves through educational catalogs such as The Learning Annex, Adult Education Center etc. Here is a list of professions that use adult education classes as a method of marketing their business:

Profession	Topics or Titles
Real Estate Professional	How To Make Enormous Profits Investing in Discounted Notes
Psychology	How To Develop a Powerful Self Esteem
Gift Basket Professional	How to Make Enormous Profits Working From Home
Writer	How To Get Rich Writing Newsletters For Others
Mortgage Broker	How To Create Financial Freedom as a Mortgage Broker
Seminar leaders	How To Develop, Promote & Market Seminars
Business Consultant	How To Make Large Profits In The Mail Order Business Working From Your Kitchen Table
Author	How To Self-Publish A Best Selling Book
Personal Fitness Trainer	How To Sell, Market & Promote Your Business To The Wealthy

Secrets of Personal Marketing Power

(This represents a very small fraction of occupations that can profit enormously teaching adult courses.) Now here is the key, and real secret, of each of the above categories on their benefits.

- Sell their products, also any books, audio and video programs they have written or produced.
- Get referrals.
- Bring memberships into their business.
- Be retained as a consultant
- Bring in new customers to their business.
- Get free publicity.
- Move old, tired and dead inventory.
- Grow their business, building profitable sales.

I hope that I've lighted that creative spark within you. In my experience I have found that just about anyone in any occupation, from Infomercials, Bed & Breakfast entrepreneurs, to exotic dancers can market successfully by teaching adult courses.

Personal Marketing Secret #11

"PROJECTING YOUR IMAGE OF EXCELLENCE."

Image is about what you are and how you position yourself or your company in the marketplace. Image is everything from your mannerisms, professionalism, integrity, talent, knowledge, to your ability to perform. Image is about everything from your stationery, business cards, brochures, newsletters, articles, interviews, advertising, marketing and sales literature, and correspondence, to the way you answer your telephone. Project your image of excellence. Creating an image is like walking a tightrope. Balancing in the middle of your marketplace with the proper image to influence the majority is not a simple task. Image is your personal marketing weapon for achieving fame, widespread

Chapter 7

public recognition, and a favorable reputation. All the personal marketing weapons you use are valuable resources in building a successful image. Great care and consideration should be taken into account when setting up and executing your marketing plans and strategies.

> **"You never get a second chance to make a first impression."** *Anonymous*

People always draw conclusions by making comparisons. If the first impression is less than desirable, it becomes more difficult to change their conclusions in the long run. On the other hand, if you've made a good first impression it's easier to sustain it. So in building your image, it's in your best interest to let people know what they should think of you and your company through your deeds and actions. People will look to your knowledge, experience, expertise, insight, and willingness to help. Projecting a strong, powerful image comes from being articulate, competent, extroverted, assertive, and ambitious. How much power and authority do you want to project? Projecting too much power and authority can have a negative effect and serious repercussions, especially if you project absolute authority which, for many, is intimidating and offensive. Some people adopt a singular approach to make an impact on others. They often feel that projecting a powerful and positive image requires using sledgehammer tactics to attract the attention of others. How wrong they are. Projecting a powerful and successful image demands control over your strong emotions. It demands acute perception, articulation and self-confidence in presenting yourself in a way that matches the desires and expectations of others. It's what I call your professional presence—that special magic that transforms a person into a personality.

Secrets of Personal Marketing Power

> "In some circumstances projecting the most effective image means being quiet, unobtrusive and apparently passive. I say apparently because what you will actually be doing is engaging in active passivity rather than being submissive. That is, your behaviour will be a matter of deliberate choice rather than unavoidable necessity."[1]

> "The other person will have a feeling about you based on that total impression. Enough of that image has to be working in your favor for you to be liked, accepted, and given what you want."[2]

---

[1]David Lewis, *The Secret Language Of Success*, page 43, Carroll & Graf, 1989.
[2]Roger Ailes, *You are the Message*, page 22, Dow Jones Irwin, 1988.

Chapter 7

> **Personal Marketing Secret #12**
>
> *"WHY PHOTO BUSINESS CARDS ARE IMPORTANT AND HOW YOU PROFIT FROM THEM."*

The traditional business cards might as well be buried six feet under the ground for all the good you get from them. However, the personal marketing full-color business card with your photograph can be a powerful, effective sales and marketing weapon. Unlike the traditional business card, a full-color photo business card tends to be passed around, not tossed out. Photo business cards will help you be more memorable if coupled with a message or information the

83

Secrets of Personal Marketing Power

recipient will gain value from and can use. Here are a few smart value ideas, to put on the back side of your card, so your customers will keep and refer to your photo business card all year.

- Motivational message to spark their creativity each day. 365 days of local merchants' discount savings (an ideal after-sale follow-up gift).
- Calendars.
- Special seasonal messages.
- Special yearly community events.
- A spiritual message.
- Sporting events schedule.

The promotional possibilities are endless if you open up your mind and be flexible and creative.

If someone hands you a card with their picture printed on it, it becomes easier for you to associate that face with a previous conversation or encounter. The purpose of your business card is for others to make contact with you easily. It should also help them in connecting with you personally, and having your photo on it can help accomplish that goal.

Be creative—your photo business card can go beyond the traditional boundaries of shape and size. My friend and colleague Lenard Baker CSP* took advantage of his last name of Baker, as in a baker of pies, for his brochure. Lenard's brochure is a rendering the same shape and size of an actual pie, folded down into a piece of pie, that can be used as a business card. It contains his selling message, photo, address, benefit message and an easy way for someone to connect with him.

Another creative and powerful way of gaining high visibility and going beyond the traditional boundaries of shape and size is to substitute your business card with a full color photo book mark.

Your personal marketing photo business cards should help support a positive self-image and send a clear message about what it is you do. For example, if you are a professional speaker, real estate agent, chiropractor, dentist, lawyer, mortgage broker, or personal fitness trainer, your card should get that message across visually without any question as to what you do.

---

*Certified Speaking Professional.

Chapter 7

They won't let go—your business card puts cash in their pockets.

Get people to hold onto your card for an entire year. Superior Business Cards, a photo business card company located in Spokane, Washington, enhance a particular card with a most unique idea. They have designed the photo "Valued Customer Card" which offers tremendous savings from local merchants who advertise on the back of your photo business card. The merchants will offer advertised discounts ranging from one dollar off of a dozen donuts, 20% off on all paint, to free dessert with any purchase of lunch or dinner. Now the real value of the card is that it is not a punch card and is designed for unlimited usage before the expiration date, most always a full year.

Presenting the card in the right way to your customers adds incredible value to the customer and to the continued relationship development. It's a smart way of letting your customer know that they are special and that you value and appreciate their business. And it's also another way of continuing to say thank you for their business.

Secrets of Personal Marketing Power

Use other peoples' business cards for your own personal marketing.

Using the same concept as the "Valued Customer Card", you can advertise on the back of others' business cards. This is smart marketing for two reasons. First, if you are the merchant who is advertising on the back side of the card, you get community-wide exposure and repeat customer sales from the person in possession of the card. Second, having the advertised merchants pass out your card benefits them as well as personally marketing you to their customers—a triple win. You get mass exposure, the advertised merchants get mass exposure and the customers get a discount on their purchase.

I pass out literally twelve to sixteen thousand photo business cards a year as a speaker. With that much exposure it is worth a nice little trade out with specialty vendors that can profit handsomely by having their company advertised on the back of my card. I can sell the space or trade out for their services and products which is what I do. Perhaps this can also be a creative and innovative opportunity for you.

Personal Marketing Secret #13

"STAY WELL CONNECTED WITH PEOPLE USING PHOTO POST CARDS."

Photo post cards are powerful marketing weapons to show your appreciation and to say thank you to your customers, colleagues and friends. Just like a personalized handwritten thank you letter, a post card is a way to communicate a sincere and meaningful message which is essential if a genuine relationship is to develop between you and your customers. Photo post cards can enhance the value of your service, and keep your customers informed of your success. Here are some excellent personal marketing strategies and ideas for using photo post cards:

Chapter 7

- Announce your new promotion.
- New product promotion.
- Special events invitation.
- Sales contest winner.
- Pre-publication of your new book.

Secrets of Personal Marketing Power

- An addition to your family.
- A new office location.
- A recent international vacation.

If you are planning a two- to four-week extended international vacation, send your customers a photo post card with you pictured in your vacation location. Upon arrival simply have your picture taken and then locate a quick print shop that can produce the photo post cards for you. Now here is a smart idea that you'll want to arrange before departing on your vacation: prepare your post card message in advance and have it typeset and ready to be printed on your post card—it will save time and money. Next, have your address labels preprinted before leaving. After you have picked up your card from the printer the only thing left to do is apply your label, stamp it, and away it goes in the mail.

Announcing your new promotion to your customers, friends, family and colleagues will focus and draw their attention to your progress and success.

Sending out photo post cards, for example, on new product promotions, a special events invitation or to announce a sales contest winner, projects a positive self-image which makes your presence felt in a most favorable way and sends a signal that conveys a successful career.

Personal marketing should be fun, exciting and at the same time meet your objectives and goals.

My own photo post card is sent to everyone who buys my books from me personally, sends me a testimonial letter, or is someone I have met on a plane, at an association meeting, or a convention, and many times I'll send a photo post card just to let people know I care about how they are doing. Also, any one attending one of my "Personal Marketing Power" seminars will receive samples of my photo post cards.

Anne Boe, a professional speaker and author of *Is Your Net-Working*, had her picture taken with Phil Donahue when she appeared on his show. Anne had the photo put on a promotional post card to be used as a marketing piece for selling her speaking engagements, book, audio and video products. Another smart personal marketing idea Anne uses is a picture of herself lying on a stack of her books, looking straight up into the camera. This picture is used in many of her promotional materials, informing more people of who and what she does.

The following are a few tips and suggestions to consider when designing your "Personal Marketing" photo post card:

- Design it around your personality.
- The design of the card should in some way reflect what it is you do.
- Design your photo post card to meet your objectives.
  a. Is the objective for personal, handwritten thank yous and notes?
  b. Are you promoting a book?
  c. Are you running a special promotion?

Be a savvy self-promoter and design your photo post card to provide a veritable campaign for enhancing and advancing your public and professional image.

Part Four
THE POWER OF
SIMPLE TRUTH

CHAPTER 8   Simple Truths in Getting
People to Believe in You

CHAPTER

8

SIMPLE TRUTHS IN GETTING PEOPLE TO BELIEVE IN YOU

Personal Marketing Secret #14

"LETTING OTHERS BLOW YOUR HORN WITH TESTIMONIAL LETTERS."

"Procrastination is opportunity's natural assassin."
Victor Kiam

Don't let up on the tension of building your Personal Marketing Power. Testimonial letters are one of your single most important power weapons available. It's the one tool that has more impact because of the power of others and what they are saying about you. Testimonial letters add to the selling power of your ads, brochures, direct mail pieces, and media kits because you can select the most powerful comments, excerpts or quotations from

Secrets of Personal Marketing Power

them for placement in your selling materials or even reprint the letters themselves.

Always have the courage to ask for testimonial letters and do it at the right moment. I've always found that the right moment for me is when someone approaches me after I've concluded my seminar or speech. The conversation generally begins with them congratulating me for my fine presentation. It's right after they have explained what incredible value and insight they received that I ask if they would be so kind as to put all that important information in writing and send it to me in a few days.

Testimonial letters work most powerfully when used with people in similar industries and company size. For example: You're in insurance sales and 50% of your business comes from Fortune 500 company Presidents and CEOs. The other 50% comes from small to medium size entrepreneurial companies. The most powerful testimonial letters used for selling to Fortune 500 companies would be letters from Presidents and CEOs of other Fortune 500 companies. The same would hold true of the smaller companies.

When promoting a seminar to the mortgage banking and mortgage brokerage industry, you don't want all your testimonials from dentists and chiropractors in your selling and promotional materials—you want testimonials from people in the mortgage industry.

> "Without question, when people are uncertain, they are more likely to use others' actions to decide how they themselves should act."
> *Robert Cialdini Ph.D.*

Like anything else in life if you want it you have to ask for it.

Chapter 8

Personal Marketing Secret #15

"REFERRALS—THE INFLUENTIAL POWER OF PEOPLE."

When we talk about referrals given by someone who is trusted and respected or with high authority, we are talking about power, raw, brutal, thrilling personal marketing power. It's always amazing to me the business that's done by referring vendors and other resources to people who are attending my seminars, workshops and speeches. I have several photo business card, post card, and video production companies as well as newsletter resources that I have contact with only once a month. Each time we talk, they report to me the amount of business that they have received from my referral of my seminar attendees to them. When I speak to groups, I become that influence and authority figure that people listen to and follow.

Several years ago I co-authored and self-published a business book entitled *The Business Of Gift Baskets—How To Make A Profit Working From Home*. In tracking our sales to assess the effectiveness of our marketing and advertising, we found that each year our greatest sales volume (the percentage of inquires converted to sales) came from another book entitled *The Best Home Businesses For The 90's* by Paul & Sarah Edwards. *The Business Of Gift Baskets* was listed in the Edwards' book as an excellent resource for people opening up a home-based gift basket business. The fact and truth of the matter is that the Edwards and their book were a credible reference for my book simply because they are viewed as authorities in home-based businesses.

The power behind referrals is that it is someone else stepping forward blowing your horn for you. The difference between your saying how good you are and a friend, client, or associate saying how good you are is like asking the difference between night and day. If you say how good you are the chances of it being believed are slimmer and less influential than if someone else says it. The exception might be if you have already established yourself as an expert in your field and are of celebrity status. Referrals can be as simple as someone dropping your name in a casual conversation, mentioning your name in a speech, or writing about you in their newsletter, magazine or book.

Robert Cialdini, Ph.D. lectures on his research and findings that one of the most potent weapons influencing others is social proof. He states:

> "The tendency to see an action as more appropriate when others are doing it normally works quite well. As a rule, we will make fewer mistakes by acting in accord with social evidence than contrary to it."[1]

One of the best methods I've found to getting a referral is to ask. There are different approaches you can use in asking for referrals. Here's how simply it works:

- When a customer says you did a terrific job, pause, look that customer in the eyes and ask, "Would you mind putting that in writing?"
- If a customer says to you, "I must tell my friends about you." pause, look that customer in the eyes and ask, "Whom specifically did you have in mind?" When the name is given to you, ask, "Would you mind calling that person on the phone and personally introducing them to me?"

Other suave approaches to obtaining referral are:

- Ask your customer to send a referral card on your behalf, recommending you based on the satisfaction you gave your customer. Have several different kinds of referral cards printed up. On the following page is a sample referral card I use after a speech.
- Mail out a customer satisfaction questionnaire. Have them fill it out. At the bottom of the page provide a permission request form for them to sign allowing you to use their

---

[1]Robert B. Cialdini, Ph.D., *Influence*, page 117, Quill, 1984.

Chapter 8

> Dear _____ , Don L. Price was our keynote
>
> speaker at our most recent regional conference, and was
>
> sensational! I endorse and highly recommend Don as a
>
> speaker for your organization, too!
>
> Sincerely, _____

name as a referral. Enclose a self addressed stamped envelope for their convenience.

- Send a handwritten Thank You follow-up letter. After giving your warm and sincere comments and appreciation for their business, write a paragraph asking them for referrals. (Note that this works more successfully if you have received positive comments from your customer first.) The paragraph could be written something like this: Now having experienced the fine results our services (products, etc.) provided, please take just a few minutes and send us the names and phone numbers of people you know who would also enjoy experiencing our services (products, etc.).

Asking for and getting referrals is one Personal Marketing Power weapon that will enhance and advance your professional presence and career. There is no business or career that is exempt from profiting from referrals. However, most people fail miserably at obtaining referrals, principally from their failure to ask for them.

> "The only conquests which are permanent,
> and leave no regrets, are our conquests
> over ourselves."   *Napoleon Bonaparte*

Secrets of Personal Marketing Power

Personal Marketing Secret #16

"HOW SMART MARKETERS GET FREE PUBLICITY BY ENDORSING OTHER PEOPLE'S PRODUCTS."

I have found a very simple way of charting new paths to the consumer and getting thousands of exposures in the marketplace. Your endorsement of other peoples' products and services can bring enormous advantages for either narrowcasting or broadcasting your service and products. We normally think of endorsements from celebrities who generally receive large sums of money for appearing in print or in the electronic media. Anyone who watches TV for any regular period of time or reads newspapers and magazines would certainly see TV and movie celebrities and famed athletes endorsing products.

But how many of you have given any thought to the value that one would receive by endorsing a book, a software product, business card manufacturer, creative paper products company or a nutritional product, for the purpose of name recognition and personal marketing? Dr. Denis Waitley, author of *The Psychology of Winning*, Anthony Robbins, author of *Unlimited Power*, Dr. Robert H. Schuller, Founder and Pastor, Crystal Cathedral, Og Mandino, author of *The Greatest Salesman in the World*, Kenneth Blanchard, Ph.D., co-author of *The One Minute Manager*, Brian Tracy, author of *Psychology of Achievement*, have all endorsed other authors' books. Authors endorsing each other's books sets up a crisscrossing effect of mass name recognition and helps in their personal marketing effort, greater sales and better distribution of their books. I have used narrowcasting, which is a fine-tuned approach to a tightly selected group of consumers, in endorsing several business card companies, and magazine and newsletter publishers. Mike Ferry, a colleague in the speaking and training business, appears in an ad for Telemagic Sales Automation Software in the inside cover of *Personal Selling Power Magazine*. Barbara Hart produced and recorded an audio cassette program entitled "Wake Up Your Brain And Be Brilliant Before

Chapter 8

Breakfast." The cover of the cassette album was designed using one of Paper Direct's products. The cover turned out to be so exceptionally unique and creative that Barbara submitted her finished product to Paper Direct in hope that they would feature it in their catalog. Paper Direct was so impressed and excited about how she had used their product that they spotlighted Barbara's audio cassette album in a special issue of their catalog.

Barbara didn't receive a large sum of cash for endorsing and allowing Paper Direct to feature her story. However, Barbara's payment came from being spotlighted in a directory that will gain her name recognition and exposure to thousands of individuals and companies with the opportunity to sell them her audio cassette program.

Think creatively and innovatively for ways in which you can take advantage of getting name recognition, sell more of your products and services, and improve your personal marketing by endorsing others' products that appear in print and the electronic media.

Personal Marketing Secret #17

"FAST-FORWARD YOUR CAREER BY SPEAKING TO GROUPS."

Secrets of Personal Marketing Power

Speaking to groups is one of the foremost and powerful personal marketing weapons you'll come across which helps you to achieve high market visibility for promoting yourself, ranking above all others. Your success in life and business will be in direct proportion to your ability to communicate your ideas, concepts, feelings, dreams and goals to other people. It doesn't matter what your current position in life is or your present level of competence right at this moment. What does matter is that your greatness comes from your willingness and ability to recognize the personal marketing power inherent in speaking to groups. Speaking is a learned skill; the benefits and extreme rewards of speaking to groups can, and will, manifest all sorts of positive opportunities for you:

- Demonstrate your leadership skills.
- Gain recognition as an expert in your profession
- Get involved in community projects.
- Win the support of others.
- Get media attention and write-ups in newspapers and magazines.
- Build your customer base.
- Promote your products and services.

How far you go will depend entirely on how seriously and rapidly you want to move forward in your career.

- Lee Iacocca took his communication skills to the people and sold America and the world on Chrysler.
- John F. Kennedy, as president of the United States, inspired a whole generation to new ways of thinking.
- Martin Luther King moved audiences with such emotion worldwide declaring, "I Have a Dream".

John F. Kennedy, Lee Iacocca, and Martin Luther King were all master communicators and tops in their field. You, too, can become a master communicator and tops in your field.

If you're a person who becomes traumatized at the thought of speaking to groups or if you had a mortifying experience the first time you stood up and gave your first presentation, you're among friends. Stage fright and other anxieties associated with speaking to groups is only normal and is experienced by the best. However,

Chapter 8

if you master and follow these four essentials—of being interesting, comfortable, committed, and most of all prepared you will possess the characteristic traits which all successful communicators possess, and your fear of speaking to groups will diminish considerably.

Don't believe for a minute that you are limited to speaking to groups assembled around a table or in an auditorium. Radio, television, video conferencing, and teleconferencing all have small to large audiences.

Know where to speak to advance your self-promotional personal marketing objectives

Every day there are thousands of group presentations, speeches, and media interviews given around the nation by individuals pursuing their unlimited promotional possibilities. Many presentations die on the spot and never meet the promotional objectives of the individual simply because the content was forgettable, or through poor promotional planning, lack of personal marketing goals, or there was no media value for local and national publicity.

The goal of any speaking engagement is to gain maximum exposure for the delivery of information about yourself, your products, services, and ideas. Maximum exposure will always include the high probability of media exposure. Speaking engagements should always include the opportunity for self-promotion. Speaking engagements should be selected based on the ability for you to realize your personal marketing goals.

Here is how to make your decision on where to speak:

- Will the group you're speaking to help promote your long-term or short-term "Personal Marketing" objectives?
  Is the audience made up of immediate client prospects?
- Is the organization, association or group important enough to the community to attract media attention for news coverage?
- Are these organizations, associations or groups affiliated or networked with other organizations, associations or groups for spin-off presentation?
- Will your presentation be newsworthy or featured in their newsletters, magazines, or bulletin board memos?

Secrets of Personal Marketing Power

- If you're making a presentation to a local branch office will it springboard you to a regional or national program?
- Is it a center of influence that needs your expertise and is asking for a favor?
- Will your presentation receive newspaper, radio or television exposure?
- Is it a presentation that will help your customer develop an account?

Time is a precious commodity—don't waste it. If you can answer these questions in the affirmative, then make the presentation. If not, consider your time investment.

Getting Invited

How do you get invited? Ask. It sounds too simple but in the beginning, if you haven't already established yourself as a expert in your field, the chances of you being invited to be a guest speaker are slim.

Here's how it works:

- Approach the program chairman of the club, association, religious organization, fraternal organization, trade or professional organization, or political organization, or your local chamber of commerce of which you are a member. If you are not a member, then ask a friend who is a member to get you an invitation.
- Provide all the necessary information to sell yourself and the benefits of your presentation and why it will be of interest to their members.
- Help the program chairman make the right decision to invite you as a guest speaker. Let the program chairman know that you will take full responsibility for preparing any advance media releases and newsletter listing that will posture the organization as one which attracts quality speakers. Explain that your media releases will let the community at large know of the good works being accomplished by the organization.

Chapter 8

- Prepare a news article for the local newspaper. Inform the program chairman that your article will include information that will give the organization some civic and professional recognition. A key point is that you will be able to bring to the attention of the general readers, and most importantly the buyers of your products and services, significant and important promotional facts about you.
- Invite the media to the program for the purpose of writing an article as a follow-up to your presentation. If the article is published, ask for copyright permission for a follow-up article for the organization's newsletter. (Important note: Be photographed with influential civic leaders and organization leaders at every venue where you speak for any follow-up article that will appear in print; add these to your credentials and media kit.)
- Call the local radio talk show stations to be interviewed on the topic you'll be presenting. Also call local community educational television programs and cable channels.

After you have made a couple of dozen speeches to your targeted market it becomes easier to be invited as a guest speaker, provided you deliver an informative, educational, problem-solving and even, perhaps, motivational or inspirational speech. Don't expect to accomplish one or two speeches and think you have conquered the world. Your goal is to always obtain additional speaking engagements and referrals from the group to which you are presently speaking. Take massive action and be guileless in the beginning. Once your momentum kicks into high speed you'll begin to recognize a pattern. First, you establish yourself as an expert. Secondly, you establish yourself as a celebrity, far more worthy of attention by the media.

Secrets of Personal Marketing Power

Personal Marketing Secret #18

"PROMOTE YOUR PRODUCT, COMPANY AND SERVICE WITH SEMINARS AND WORKSHOPS."

Use seminars to obtain bookings, consulting, leads, referrals, and product sales. If you do not market and sell your products, services, and company through public seminars and workshops, you may be losing out on an extremely cost-effective way to:

- Increase your professional presence and public image.
- Increase your customer base.
- Triple product sales.
- Build an effective lead-generating system.

Seminars and workshops are an alternative to cold calls, direct mail, or other kinds of marketing. Many companies and individuals use seminars to market and sell products and services: banks, mortgage companies, insurance companies, computer firms, consultants, real estate promoters, law firms that offer living trust seminars, and chiropractors who offer free seminars to build a strong customer base. Today almost all services and products can be marketed through seminars and workshops.

One company that I was a seminar speaker for used seminars to sell their consulting services. Their service did not have a broad base mass market appeal, so we had to create a highly successful and different approach to obtaining new clients. We worked on the premise that marketing our services through seminars creates a high-quality lead-generating system to obtain new clients, and our seminars were also designed as a profit center. To accomplish this, we set three major objectives:

1. Offer a profitable selling seminar with high content and valuable information for which we could charge a fee.

Chapter 8

2. Sell high-quality education materials at the seminar.
3. Convert our seminar attendees into clients as an after-sale at the seminar, and/or sell additional educational materials.

To accomplish these goals successfully and with regular frequency required a flexible system and experimental approach to our targeted and niche market.

The following are five key ideas for the success of that company's marketing through seminars:

a. We promoted heavily in newspapers. Copy and placement of our ads were more critical than size. (Big is not always better.)
b. The frequency of seminars in major metropolitan areas was every 90 days, to produce maximum attendance. Fewer days in between literally cut attendance to less than half. Over 90 days bore no significant increase.
c. The location of hotels where we held the seminars had a serious impact on having a large or small turnout. (In New York commuters use subways. Downtown Manhattan draws a larger group than a venue at either Kennedy or La Guardia Airport.)
d. Selling a high-priced set of educational materials at the seminars dramatically increased dollar profits and sales volume, and gave us better pre-qualified leads for selling our consulting services.

Seminars and workshops are key personal marketing weapons, as well as a source of income. However, not everyone gives seminars and workshops as a direct source of income, that is, to make a profit from attendees' fees or product sales at the seminar. For example, a tax consultant is motivated to offer seminars as a way of building the business. Xerox ensures its own future by offering free educational seminars and workshops to their customers. Offering free customized training courses to their customers on technical, marketing and management skills helps ensure the success and profitability of those customers. A manufacturer of paint products offers seminars and workshops to their retailers on selling skills and product safety. Staples, the office

Secrets of Personal Marketing Power

superstore, hired an outside trainer to offer seminars and workshops on customer service programs. Those sessions were held on site at different Staples store locations for their retail customers, free of charge. A major stock brokerage firm of national repute targets middle-class to upper-middle-class couples to attend a free seminar on tax-sheltering and investment strategies. After the couples spent several hours listening to experts on their subjects, the attendees were invited to one-on-one private conversations.

Mortgage & title companies will often sponsor my seminar "Personal Marketing Power" for the real estate professionals as a marketing strategy for positioning their companies in the forefront of the real estate community.

Many companies that use seminars for marketing will sponsor experts in a particular discipline as their seminar or workshop leader. Many times they will do this not because the sponsoring company doesn't have the expertise themselves, but because good presentations require skills other than just being an expert on the subject. The information superhighway has arrived and good presentations require skills in using computer technology. Computer graphics, slides, overheads, videos and music are changing the form of seminars and workshops, making them take on a more entertainment or educational atmosphere, and immersing the audience in a more interactive program. However don't let this be a roadblock to your personal marketing—look at it as a real opportunity.

Promoting public seminars and workshops that are primarily designed to obtain new customers presents a somewhat higher risk simply because you're depending on your form of advertising to pull a large attendance, whereas the in-house customer seminar that Staples promotes has less risk.

The Magic Marketing Rule of Success

To achieve success you must accurately define your target market. The key rule of promoting successful seminars and workshops is to go where your audience is or to work with people who have a captive audience waiting for you. Without a doubt,

Chapter 8

you'll need to identify your target market and you'll accomplish that by designing a concise and efficient marketing plan.

That plan must include the following considerations and questions:

- Identify the potential customers that will make up your audience—your primary market.
- Consider if there is a secondary market for your services and products.
- What selling tactics will be employed to influence your audience to buy?
- How will you test market your seminar or workshop?
- What kind of dollar investment will you be committed to?
- What additional products are planned for after the initial roll-out?
- What guideline will you use to measure results and success?
- Identify the best method of bringing your target audience to your seminar (i.e., direct mail, newspaper advertising, unsponsored seminars and workshops, or sponsored presentations).
- If self-sponsored and using direct mail, what list will you use? (i.e., existing customer list, compiled list, income bracket list, selected industry list, etc.).
- Direct mail marketing brochure style, layout, color, content, fold, size.
- Will your seminar require radio and newspaper advertising support?
- Will you mail first class or bulk rate? You'll need to take into consideration your lead time to get the maximum number of attendees.
- Location of seminar and time.
- Will refreshments be served? If so, what kind—coffee, tea, pastries, a full-course meal?
- What audiovisual equipment will be needed?
- What staffing support will be required?
- What seminar handouts will be required?

Keep in mind that the success of your seminar or workshop rests in the function of marketing and promotion in getting it off

Secrets of Personal Marketing Power

the ground. However, the ultimate success is the result of program content, the value to your targeted audience, and your instructional and platform competency.

Personal Marketing Secret #19

"THANK YOU NOTES & LETTERS BUILD LASTING AND POWERFUL RELATIONSHIPS."

The fastest way to kill relationships is to never acknowledge and appreciate the value of another person. On the other hand, the fastest way you build and allow relationships to take root, grow and bloom is to always acknowledge the value of the relationship and show your appreciation by sending thank you notes. Sending a thank you note can generate enormous influence in getting other people to like you. The harsh reality is that if you are entering into a relationship looking for and expecting some kind of special treatment, you'll only receive it after you have demonstrated selfless action and care for the other person. Sending thank you notes can help you accomplish that goal. The act of sending thank you notes also rallies people to your cause and lets them experience a part of your success.

Below is a way of saying thank you that broadcasts your success.

Dear _____,

Today represents a special moment in my life that I would like to share with you. I have just been awarded top salesperson of the year. I want you to know that winning the award was partly due to your encouragement and advice. Thank you,

Don

Chapter 8

The essence of your Personal Marketing Power is enabling as many people as possible to participate in your vision and growth. Remember, the first principle of Personal Marketing Power is "it's who you know and who knows you that brings you success in life." Find every reason possible for sending thank you notes but avoid superficiality.

Personal Marketing Secret #20

"YOUR MARKETING KIT IS YOUR TOP COAT TO SUCCESS."

The artist uses paint on a canvas to express a feeling, make a statement, and create an illusion to move the viewer. The writer uses words as tools to persuade, motivate, evoke emotion, create mental pictures, entertain and educate the reader. You have your Personal Marketing Power marketing kit to persuade your readers that you have something of value to offer. Who needs a marketing kit? You do, if you are serious about your professional presence and about promoting yourself as a guest on radio or television, getting write-ups in newspapers and magazines or booking yourself as a guest speaker. Appearing on radio and cable or public television can be great way to promote your book, promote a fund raiser, or promote your company's product or idea. You would also send out your marketing kit to newspapers and magazines that want to do a story on you, and companies, associations, organizations, schools, and universities that are considering hiring you as a speaker or to conduct a workshop or seminar. Now that you're ready to become a self-proclaimed self-promoting whiz, you'll need to carefully prepare your marketing kit to get you the attention and exposure you need and deserve. What you need in the way of a marketing kit will definitely depend a great deal on what you are trying to accomplish and to whom you'll be sending your kit. For example, if you've been asked to send your marketing kit to one of the major network talk

Secrets of Personal Marketing Power

shows to promote your new product, any materials or testimonials you have from your local TV/Radio or newspapers should certainly be included.

Here are the components that make up your marketing kit:

Chapter 8

Biographical information.
Media release (press release).
Photographs.
Previous media appearances and articles.
Public service/Calendar announcements.
Books you have written.
Testimonial letters.
Company brochure.
Cover letter.
Video or audio demo tapes.

After you have assembled your marketing kit material, place it in a quality pocket folder. The type of folder I've used is made by DUO-TANG® stock #50425, with a slick gloss finish. They can be purchased in a variety of colors and also in black & white. On the outside of the folder I simply adhere one of my photo post cards to give it instant identity and a professional appearance.

Your Biographical information

Part of your Personal Marketing strategy is to provide a well-written biographical background history of yourself for use in your media releases, conferences and events. Here are the guidelines for writing and formatting your bio:

- Write your bio in a "feature story" format consisting of 250 to 400 words.
- Have an attention-getting first paragraph that hooks or compels the reader to be interested in reading more about you. This paragraph should also answer the reader's question: Why would someone want to interview me?
- The second paragraph is the supporting data that portrays your personality and characteristics, and will include quotations about you. This is where the writer in you uses words as tools that are engaging, evoke emotion and create mental pictures to let the reader see you as you are.
- The third paragraph shows substance matter which will establish you as a person of significant worth or value. This is where your mastery and your technical competency is clearly presented.

111

Secrets of Personal Marketing Power

- In the subsequent paragraphs include personal information such as your age, marital status, children, hobbies, and sports in which you're active. Add any personal or witty information with a mixture of additional hard facts and quotations that would help embellish and create human interest.

Media release (Press release)

You want your media release to read exactly as you would like the reporter to write it. Your media release should be composed of no more than 450 to 500 words, double-spaced, with approximately 250 words per page. Write your media release in story form supplying facts and specific information on the person, product or event taking place. Make sure you answer all the who, what, where, when and why questions. Use only one side of the paper. If your release extends to two pages, at the bottom of the first page write the word "more". At the top of the second page write the word "continue"—type your headline in caps and indicate Page 2 of 2. At the end of your release type the word "end".

Photographs

Send your photograph with every media release and always include it in your media kit. Your photograph should be 5" x 7" or 8" x 10" in size and in black and white (however, some magazines and newspapers are using color. Check this out before sending). The traditional photograph is a head and shoulder shot, unless it is a gala event and then you may want to use a full figure shot.Don't write on the back of your photograph or use paper clips to attach notes.

Have a label made which includes:

- Complete names of those pictured.
- Complete details if it's an event picture.
- Follow-up information, fax and phone number.

Previous media appearances & print media clips

Photocopy all your previous publicity announcements, newspaper and magazine articles you have written, and articles written about you for distribution in your marketing kit. There are several

Chapter 8

ways to prepare the articles. You can photocopy the articles as they appear in print onto your business stationery. Have them repositioned and printed on quality 8 1/2" x 11" white linen or color paper stock with your information printed at the end.

On your business stationery list all the radio or network shows and any other electronic media where you have appeared.

- List the name of the program.
- List the date the program was on the air.
- The city and state.
- The station and station call letters.
- The name of the producer and the host of the program.

Your public service/Calendar announcements

Your local radio stations and newspapers announce upcoming special events, fund raisers, seminars, and any number of community projects. Public service announcements are aired through the electronic media and calendar announcements are published in the print media. On your stationery type and double-space your public service and calendar announcements to include the following information:

- Name, address, and telephone number of your organization.
- The name of the event sponsor(s) and contact person(s).
- Include any price of admission.
- Write out your announcement not to exceed 50 words in length and 30 seconds for the announcer to read over the air.
- Your announcement needs to be sent 2 to 3 weeks in advance of the event.

Note: Radio/TV stations and print publications have widely different policies regarding public service and calendar announcements. Therefore, it's always best to contact the public service director for the electronic media and calendar editor for print media for the correct policies and procedures.

Books you have written

If you are being interviewed on a network talk show or radio program definitely send your book to be reviewed by the pro-

Secrets of Personal Marketing Power

gram host prior to your appearance. However, unless otherwise requested I normally have additional book covers printed for inclusion in my marketing kit.

Testimonial letters

I've already discussed earlier in this book that testimonial letters are one of your single most important power weapons available. It's the one tool that has more impact because of the power of others and what they are saying about you. Testimonial letters add to the selling power of your ads, brochures, direct mail pieces and media kits. Use them always!

Video or audio demo tapes

Video and audio demos have been used extensively and almost exclusively by speakers for marketing themselves to meeting planners, conventions, associations, on-site seminars and work-shops. Video and audio tapes have become a major personal marketing weapon in all types of industries. Real estate, mort-gage, insurance, medical, health and nutritional, computer, and network marketing to mention a few have prospered using videos and audio tapes in their direct mail marketing campaigns. A high-quality video and audio demo can open doors of oppor-tunity for promoting yourself, your products, and for getting media coverage. When considering having a video or audio demo produced, select an experienced company that understands what your industry needs and how best to sell your message.

Always develop any of the Personal Marketing Weapons that will be representing you in the market place to look, feel and sound like good quality.

> **Aristotle said it best. "Quality is not an act.
> It is a habit."**

Part Five

MORE POWER WEAPONS

CHAPTER 9 Smart Ideas that Work

CHAPTER 10 Put Your Mind to Work on Creativity, Imagination and Innovation

CHAPTER

9

SMART IDEAS
THAT WORK

Personal Marketing Secret #21

"THE POWER OF UNSOLICITED TESTIMONIALS."

This is a bonanza of an idea that I learned from Dan Kennedy, Empire Communications Corp. located in Phoenix, AZ. It takes an innovative and creative maverick marketer like Dan Kennedy to pull this off. It's so simple it borders on brilliance. However, I have expanded this unique concept and marketing strategy. The application of using the unsolicited testimonial is enormous. This marketing strategy can be applied to any professional organization, industry, company, association, fund raiser, product or service. Here is how Dan applied this unique concept. Dan Kennedy is a consultant, speaker and author. He has authored numerous books, audio and video programs of which he markets and sells through his seminars, direct mail marketing, book stores and various other channels of distribution. In a new product

---

117

Secrets of Personal Marketing Power

offering sent to his current customers, Dan inserted a separate page offering an extra $50.00 discount for anyone whose name appeared on the list. He listed his customers alphabetically and across from their name listed their business or what it was they had accomplished.

For example: His attention-getting headline at the top of the page was a statement that read:

Thanks to repetitive purchases of my materials, attending my seminar, utilizing my consulting services, etc., the people on this list are entitled to an extra $50.00 discount

Under the heading he listed all of his customers in this manner:

Leeds, Dorothy   Author, *Smart Questions*
Price, Don L.   Speaker/Author, *The Secrets of Personal Marketing Power*

At the bottom of the page you could make another statement indicating to those listed that if their name appears on the list they are entitled to deduct $50.00 or some other amount from the purchase of your offering. Also you can make another statement that if anyone felt left off the list to call for authorization to obtain their discount.

The power employed in this marketing strategy is that it capitalizes on the influence principle of people proof—meaning that others like yourself have purchased, therefore you must have made a smart decision in your purchase.

This marketing strategy is a classic way to grow your business. To the best of my knowledge and business experience, there are only three ways to grow any business.

- First, you can increase the number of times a customer buys from your business.
- Second, you can increase your dollar amount per sale per customer.
- Third, you can increase your number of customers.

The smart business person is marketing to all three customer categories. Use the unsolicited testimonial creatively in your

Chapter 9

power marketing. If you are a big user of direct mail marketing, have a newsletter, or use seminars to market your services or products—the unsolicited testimonial can effectively be used on all your printed materials. Here are some possible ideas to stimulate your thinking for chasing new business and increasing your customer base using direct mail.

For a photographer your headline could read:

"Picture Perfect"
That's what all these customers tell us.

After that headline list 30 to 50 of your customers' names.

For a seminar promoter your headline could read:

"One Step Ahead of the Competition"
That's what these people had an opportunity to achieve after attending our Peak Performers Seminar

After that headline list 150 to 300 names.

For a Fund Raiser your headline could read:

As a way of saying Thank You to our Gold Club annual contributors for helping us meet our fund raising goal three years in a row—those fine people listed will receive a special certificate of recognition for their contribution this year.

List the Gold Club contributors after that headline.

Think and be innovative and creative in selecting and implementing ways of utilizing the unsolicited testimonial.

Secrets of Personal Marketing Power

Personal Marketing Secret #22

"HELP SUPPORT YOUR CUSTOMERS' CAUSES."

Support your customers with articles of information that you have clipped from newspapers, magazines, and trade journals that would be of value in helping them improve their life and careers. Savvy marketers go above and beyond good customer service. Excellence is their order of the day. Be inquisitive and an information gatherer about your customers' career goals, lifestyle goals and educational goals. Create a people contact management system where you can easily store and retrieve information instantly about your customers. Nurture your customers always and as the relationship builds and grows continue to update your information files on your customers. When you clip information or ideas from print publications, take the additional time to copy it onto your stationery along with attaching your picture photo business card to it. Many times clipped information that you send your customers will either get posted on a bulletin board or passed on to others to read. Having your picture on the clipping says that you're the source of information and gives you broader exposure within your customer's organization. After all, that's what a savvy personal marketer does—get more exposure to increase the chance of opportunity presenting itself. There is nothing wrong in creating a little thunder and being recognized as someone who goes beyond good customer service.

> "Thunder is good, thunder is impressive, but it is the lightning that does the work."   *Mark Twain*

Chapter 9

Personal Marketing Secret #23

"SHREWD MARKETING WITH VIDEO BROCHURES."

Smart marketers are connecting with their buyers through a variety of different marketing mediums. However, the shrewd marketers are tenaciously going out after their customers with the visual electronic media which includes the use of video brochures. What is a video brochure? It's a video tape containing a promotional selling message about your services, products, and company. The information in a video brochure is designed to lure your prospective or current customers to buy your offering. A video brochure can be more compelling and dramatically influencing than a written brochure. Video brochures will be 7 to 15 minutes in length. A commercial on television represents a very short version (30 seconds to 60 seconds) of a video brochure. An infomercial would be an extended version of a video brochure. The video brochure is a real show-and-tell marketing tool that allows you to have customer testimonials or live-action demonstrations of your products or services, and literally appeal and play to the emotions of your viewers. Videos have been used primarily as sales and marketing tools by companies with large advertising budgets. Because of the production cost of a video, many companies and individuals simply could not afford their own video. However, today it is becoming a favorable marketing tool because of low production cost and an effective high quality product.

Use a video brochure in your sales and personal marketing strategy in the following ways:

- Leave behind for your prospective customer.
- In newspapers, magazines, radio and TV ads, have the potential for customers to call for their free video for more information.
- Direct response mail program.

Secrets of Personal Marketing Power

- Use at trade shows and conventions.
- Shopping malls and retail outlets.
- As an educational video in doctor, dentist and chiropractic offices.

Who can use a personal marketing video brochure?

- Speakers
- Loan agents
- Real estate agents
- Personal Fitness trainers
- Consultants
- Trainers
- Insurance agents
- Medical professionals

Marketing with a video brochure can be varied and creative, from speakers selling themselves to a meeting planner, to a prospective employee climbing the corporate ladder.

Personal Marketing Secret #24

"AUDIO BROCHURES PUT YOU ON THE LEADING EDGE OF YOUR INDUSTRY."

An audio brochure, or as it is more commonly referred to in the speaking industry, an audio demonstration tape, is one of many marketing weapons used for booking a speaking engagement. For a professional speaker to compete for paid speaking engagements, they must at the very least have an audio demo tape that a meeting planner can listen to for making a hiring decision. Your speaker's audio demo tape should preferably be recorded from a live presentation that demonstrates your professional ability as a speaker. An audio demo tape used in the speaking industry will have a running time of seven to ten minutes utilizing the speaker's best material.

The audio brochure is designed and developed with the same

Chapter 9

goal as the audio demo tape, which is to sell your products or services. However, the length can vary from seven to thirty minutes with the optimal time being ten to fourteen minutes.

The audio brochure can literally put you on the leading edge in your industry in your sales and marketing with direct response mail, inquiry ads and other print or electronic advertising.

The audio brochure contains your selling message or offering to a prospective customer.

A quality audio tape is produced in a studio with music and a professional introduction by an announcer, followed by your offering and calls for action at the close.

A smart personal marketing idea is to personalize your audio tape. There are several way of personalizing your tapes. One is, when recording at the studio, to leave a sixty second "blank" in the beginning of your audio brochure. This allows you to insert the tape into your own cassette recorder and record a custom message for the prospective customer before sending it out.

One company with which I've been associated for many years has successfully used audio brochures to sell a business opportunity program. An audio brochure is just like the video brochure and is designed to lure your prospective or current customers into buying your offering.

However, the audio brochure generally is more in line with the budget of smaller companies and those individuals that are just starting out marketing themselves.

Audio brochures are the perfect marketing weapon for:

- Fund raising projects
- Real estate agents
- Loan agents
- Gift basket designers
- Business opportunity sales
- Insurance agents
- Medical professionals
- Professional Speakers
- Seminar and workshop promoters
- Personal Fitness trainers
- Sports therapists
- Campaigning or lobbying

Secrets of Personal Marketing Power

Savvy personal marketing is sometimes doing something different. Smart marketing requires innovation and creativity. Audio brochures are for people who are fearless in their marketing and have a clear vision of what it is they are chasing after. The audio brochure helps them to accomplish their task.

Personal Marketing Secret #25

"USE TEAM MARKETING FOR PROPELLING YOUR BUSINESS TO GREATER SUCCESS."

Team marketing is forming a strategic alliance with others in both similar or dissimilar industries and professions. Successful team marketing can lead to more business, expand your marketing base and reduce expense because of shared cost. A real estate agent can team up with a loan agent and title insurance representative and form an alliance for mutual benefit. All three deal with the same customer in the purchase of real estate. You could add to that list numerous other professionals such as a lawyer, property and casualty insurance agent, and pest control company. Jointly they can market through home buyers' seminars and workshops, advertising specialty items and direct response mail programs.

Personal Fitness trainers can team market with a nutritionist and a fitness equipment company.

A graphic artist can team market with a writer and printer.

Speakers can team market with other speakers as well as with vendors. As a how-to author, I team market and sell through industry specific vendors and merchants. They become dealer drop-ship partners in the sale and distribution of my products to their customers through their catalogues, and I advertise and promote their products and services in the distribution of products to my customers. The vendor can advertise my product in their catalogues with little or no increase in cost, which helps them

124

Chapter 9

have a larger dollar sale per customer. I reciprocate by fulfilling the orders without any advertising or direct marketing cost, which gives me a higher profit.

Be creative in looking for ways that you can team market with others to increase visibility, name recognition and boost your business.

Personal Marketing Secret #26

"PERSONALIZED INFORMATION LETTERS—STAYING WELL-CONNECTED TO YOUR CUSTOMERS BRINGS PROFITS."

Stay well-connected to your customers by sending a personalized information letter on how you and your business are doing. A one page letter briefly outlining the past year's events, your personal activities and business accomplishments, written with a personal touch similar to chit-chat or a gossip sheet works wonders. You'll not only surprise your customers with such consideration for thinking about them, you'll actually astonish them. Sending out letters to your customers makes them feel special and they appreciate that you would include them in your personal life. Personal letters help bond the customer relationship for future business opportunities.

> "Small opportunities are often the beginning of great enterprises." *Demosthenes*

In addition to sending out a personalized letter once a year you should also inform your customers of any awards or promotions you have received, books you have written, community programs you have participated in or any other important activity you may have been involved with that demonstrates an upward spiral in your career. Remember that in personal marketing, you are always selling others on who you are and what you do, in a way that doesn't appear to braggadocio.

Peter Lowe, an international speaker who mixes sales and faith on the platform, sends out letters several times a year to people who have attended his presentations. Peter shares the platform with such notables as the Rev. Robert Schuller, motivational speaker Zig Ziglar, gold medalist Mary Lou Retton and Desert Storm Commander Gen. H. Norman Schwarzkopf. My dear friend Will Grant, who is in the mortgage business, sends out a nice handwritten post card attached to an announcement from his company showing him as one of the top five producers who has won an all expense paid trip for one week to Hawaii.

I'll send out thousands of photo post cards or letters announcing the publication of this book to many seminar attendees, close friends, associates and people who have purchased other products from my company in the past. As a result of keeping these people informed, I'll receive hundreds of book orders.

It may appear that by using this form of personal marketing you are always lobbying for others to support your cause and the truth of the matter is you are. Anyone who truly understands how important and valuable marketing is will become a master at finding ways of connecting positively with their customers. That is truly the optimistic approach to chasing the business and grabbing the opportunities flying your way. Opportunity is waiting for you, but you have to make it happen.

> "I've never seen a monument erected to a pessimist."   *Paul Harvey*

> "When one door of opportunity closes, another opens; but often we look so long at the closed door that we do not see the one which has been opened for us."   *Helen Keller*

CHAPTER 10

PUT YOUR MIND TO WORK ON CREATIVITY, IMAGINATION AND INNOVATION

Creativity, imagination and innovation is the triad that's the most powerful weapon for achievement and bringing about greatness in your life and career.

Creativity is more than being a master architect who designs elaborate buildings or a master artist like Michelangelo, who painted the ceiling of the Sistine Chapel. Creativity is much more than a fashion designer creating an exquisite clothing line or a musician so eloquently putting sounds to the lyrics of a song. Creativity is about combining thoughts, methods and ideas together to bring about a more productive and harmonious life style. Creativity occurs when you find ways of connecting things together in different ways that allow you to move forward positively and productively. Creativity is a process that enables you to see things from a different perspective, bringing about possibilities and change. Imagination is part of the creative process that brings out the visual images of what might be if we were to discard the information we hold in our mind as real. A perfect example would be that of the telephone, once known as an instrument that allowed only a two-way conversation. Today the telephone goes beyond just two-party communi-

Secrets of Personal Marketing Power

cations. Computers have capabilities that boggle the mind of many who lack vision and imagination. Your imagination can come up with dazzling insights and images that can produce startling innovation. Using imagination and visual imagery has helped people overcome illness, improved the performance of athletes and improved financial opportunities.

Innovation is moving forward with your creative and imaginative "out-flow" to bring about new and improved products and services. Innovation generally occurs when people feel passionate or are on a mission, and flourishes when encouraged.

Creativity and imagination are partly inborn, partly developed by training and both are valuable and essential in carrying through your personal marketing.

> "Innovation has never come through bureaucracy and hierarchy. It's always come from individuals."   *John Sculley*

Put your mind to work coming up with ideas on how you can develop some real magic in your marketing. Be observant of things around you and look for possibilities and innovative ideas for building your personal marketing.

> "If you don't expect the unexpected, you will never find it."   *Jurgen Moltmann*

Always think ahead and look at things from a different perspective to find the unexpected. Rarely do we look to our competition for profiting in our business and that can be a major mistake. How often have you thought of having your customers or another company sponsor and promote your business? Opportunities are lurking in the shadows of others—yes, even your competitors.

Try This:

1. Look for ways you can profit from your competition. One way would be to exchange the customer mailing list that

Chapter 10

you haven't had success selling for your competitor's customer mailing list that they haven't been able to sell.

List two ideas of your own:

1. _____

2. _____

2. Have other companies promote and sponsor you. If you're a personal fitness trainer, have a community hospital promote and sponsor your seminar.

List three ideas of your own:

1. _____

2. _____

3. _____

Is an infomercial a good marketing weapon for you? If so, how? Have you looked around your community for opportunities that would support your personal marketing efforts? Advertising on grocery carts is a smart marketing idea many use to boost their chances of obtaining new customers in their communities.

The combination of creativity, imagination, innovation and the courage to act on personal marketing is your passport to propelling yourself to greater personal and business success. As Francis Bacon said, "A wise man will make more opportunities than he finds."

Part Six
YOUR POWER PLAN

CHAPTER 11 Building Your
"Personal Marketing Power"

CHAPTER 11

BUILDING YOUR
PERSONAL MARKETING POWER

First Things First!

Don't Be Held Hostage By Your Excuses

A very wise and wealthy person once told me "that most people wake up every morning finding reasons why things don't work—yielding many opportunities for others. Their whole frame of thought is immersed in statements that bear excuses for not accomplishing more in life, all of which are generally brought about by their conditioning and myths that they believe in."

Look deeply into your own life at the excuses holding you hostage from accomplishing more of your opportunities. Be brutally honest with yourself as you write them down.

_____

_____

_____

_____

Secrets of Personal Marketing Power

_____

_____

Next, write down ways to free yourself from these excuses.

_____

_____

_____

_____

_____

Now write down what will happen to you when you rid yourself of all the excuses you have listed.

What will you become? What will you have in:

One Year: _____

_____

_____

Two Years: _____

_____

_____

Five Years: _____

_____

_____

Chapter 11

Embody Passion, Insight and Vision

What are you passionate about? What is it that you believe in so much that you are willing to make a major commitment to manifesting it in your life?

Forgetting about all your excuses of:

"I'm too old."
"I'm too young."
"I'm too poor."
"It's too late."
"I'm not educated well enough."
"It's not the right time."
"I have a family to look out for."
"I don't live in the right location."

I'm sure they all sound too familiar—I'm not trying to sound pompous—God only knows I have been there, too.

The truth of the matter is that in the global arena where we live and play every day of our lives offers ample opportunity for each of us and it's only getting better and bigger.

Write down everything that comes to mind that (if you had no excuses not to) you would passionately chase after and want to give your heart and soul to accomplish.

_____

_____

_____

_____

_____

_____

_____

Secrets of Personal Marketing Power

Open up to your ideas and vision. We all have insight, but what's even more illuminating is to look around at what people are doing in this world to acquire wealth and happiness. This country still offers the best opportunity for people to experience their greatness. After all, we live in a land of plenty. You don't have to be a Bill Gates, Ted Turner or a Donald Trump to be successful. I remember my dad telling me many times that "there are more big fishes in little ponds than there are big fishes in big ponds." He was stressing the point that opportunity is opulent and all around regardless of the size of the pond you're in. Bill Gates, Ted Turner and Donald Trump happen to be the big fishes in the big pond.

Write out your mission statement. You'll soon recognize which pond you'll be swimming in. By the way, it doesn't matter which pond you end up in because both have incredibly unlimited opportunities.

_____

_____

_____

_____

_____

_____

_____

Time To Take Inventory

Let's take a reality check about what's most important for someone becoming a winner.

1. Charm and personality is an enormous asset for becoming a winner. The following all possess enormous charm and personality.

Chapter 11

- Presidents Kennedy, Reagan, and Clinton
- Sports celebrities Magic Johnson and Mary Lou Retton
- Business personalities Harvey Mackay, Connie Chung, Valerie Salembier, and Herb Kelleher

Write down three people that inspire you with their personality.

1. _____

2. _____

3. _____

2. Don't worry about being too young or too old. Age is irrelevant to success.

- Bill Gates of Microsoft wasn't worried about being too young.
- Ray Kroc, at 52, didn't let age stand between him and creating McDonald's.

3. Powerful resources and connections are prime assets for becoming a success in life.

- Donald Trump's seed money reportedly came from his father.
- Harvey Mackay has been well-connected with the right people through the Chamber of Commerce, Young Presidents Organization, past association with the Minnesota Twins and many more.

There is one key asset all of the above mentioned personalities have in common for achieving their greatness in life. They've all been great marketers.

4. Write down all of your positive sources of support, including friends, family, associates, and competitors.

_____

_____

Secrets of Personal Marketing Power

_____

_____

_____

5. List all of the organizations, associations, business groups and clubs of which you're a member that you can tap into for additional resources and information. (Information is power if used correctly.) If you're not a member of any organization, association, group or club, then start listing those that can help build-up you and your career.

_____

_____

_____

_____

_____

6. List your assets and liabilities. Under assets, list the things you're really good at and enjoy doing. Under liabilities, list the things you're not good at and that keep you from moving ahead and capturing those opportunities smacking you in the face everyday. Find ways to turn your liabilities into assets. (It's been said that Ray Kroc couldn't plan a menu but he built an empire).

_____

_____

_____

_____

_____

Chapter 11

Masterminding Your Personal Marketing Plan

Building a bigger network

Write out a plan for building a bigger network. We all need to grow our people base and establish relationships to increase our opportunities of accomplishing our goals.

List five people whose help you want to solicit as a mentor or adviser in developing your Personal Marketing. Select people that have been successful at what it is you want their help and advice on.

1. _____

2. _____

3. _____

4. _____

5. _____

Your Personal Marketing campaign

Write out a concise personal marketing campaign. Will it include print and electronic media? Will it include seminars, workshops and public speaking? Are you going to have a direct response mail program? Be aggressive and committed to staying on track and on time.

Pencil in a rough outline now.

_____

_____

_____

_____

_____

Secrets of Personal Marketing Power

_____

_____

Is a book in your future plans?

Will you self-publish? What will your book be about? Have you a title for your book? Write your answers now to all those questions.

_____

_____

_____

_____

Your Marketing Team

Select your marketing team—I'm referring here to the various vendors and resources you'll need to help in the development and carrying out of your Personal Marking plan. List all of the vendors, resources and people you'll call upon, such as photographers, writers, graphic designers, printers, outside consultants and others who are experienced in areas that will assist in your development.

Pencil in some ideas now—you can detail it out later.

_____

_____

_____

_____

_____

_____

_____

Chapter 11

Organize and Evaluate

Organize your plan and constantly evaluate your progress.

- Evaluate who your potential customers are.

List your potential customers by ranking them in order from 1 being greatest potential to 5 being of lesser potential.

1. _____

2. _____

3. _____

4. _____

5. _____

- What makes you and your product or service more desirable than that of your competition?

List five desirable reasons that make you, your product or service better that your competition.

1. _____

2. _____

3. _____

4. _____

5. _____

- Who is making a major contribution to your success?

List three people who are making a major contribution to your success.

1. _____

2. _____

3. _____

Secrets of Personal Marketing Power

- Which strategies and methods are working best for you and are most successful in yielding a high return in your investment of time and money?

List five of your best strategies and methods.

1. _____

2. _____

3. _____

4. _____

5. _____

Stepping Into Your Plan Of Action

After you have created you master personal marketing plan you need to literally step into your plan and take action. You need to focus on your plan and your ideas and don't let up on the tension of following through. Waiting for the perfect plan to materialize will only result in procrastination. The one thing you can be absolutely sure of is that your plan will change in the process.

Also, as you share your plan with others, beware. Unless you chose to be associated with people who are supportive of your plans, you can expect to be bombarded with negatives.

Here are some antidotes for staying focused on your plan:

- Surround yourself with quality people who share in your plan.
- Read success stories and biographies of individuals that come from a background similar to yours, and of those who endured hardships in the process of achieving their greatness.
- Turn off your negative self-talk and turn on your positive self-talk.
- Recognize and understand that chances are you'll have more failure than success.
- Set an appointment each day with yourself to work on your personal marketing.

Chapter 11

- Celebrate the little wins and victories every day.
- Be so committed and so passionate that you become unstoppable.

> "I can't imagine a person becoming a success who doesn't give this game of life everything he's got."   *Walter Cronkite*

> "A man would do nothing if he waited until he could do it so well that no one could find fault."   *John Henry Newman*

> "Failure is a disappointment but not a defeat."
> *Jeanne Robertson*

Secrets of Personal Marketing Power

Don's Ten Commandments for Developing Your Personal Marketing Power

- Create your own luck by being prepared when opportunity presents itself.
- Be creative, innovative and fearless in your Personal Marketing.
- Treat and build every relationship as a long-term investment.
- Change & challenge are the order of the day—be flexible.
- Stay well-connected to people that will push or pull you to your golden destination.
- Always give more of yourself in every aspect of your life.
- Seize the moment and the opportunities, and empower yourself through the power and synergy of people.
- Don't let others destroy your dreams—create positive sources of support for your goals.
- Create a greater vision of yourself for yourself.
- Every day, apply the principles of "Secrets of Personal Marketing Power."

Part Seven

APPENDIX RESOURCES

RESOURCES

Video Production

Creative Media Resources
David Jacobson
712 Bancroft Rd., Suite 264
Walnut Creek, CA 94598
800-366-4239
510-945-9378
Fax 510-932-3017
Media Consulting, Video Production, Television, Promotion

Chesney Communications
Robert Chesney
2302 Martin St., Suite 125
Irvine, CA 92715
800-223-8878
Fax 714-263-5506
Media Consulting, Video Production, Television

Photo Business Card Companies

Daicolo Corporation
21203 A Hawthorne Blvd.
Torrance, CA 90503
310-543-2700
800-772-9993
Fax 310-316-7867

Secrets of Personal Marketing Power

Superior Business Cards
8025 N. Division, Suite F
Spokane, WA 99208
800-745-9565
Fax 509-467-9572

Photo Post Card Companies

Daicolo Corportion
21203 A Hawthorne Blvd.
Torrance, CA 90503
310-543-2700
800-772-9993
Fax 310-316-7867

Superior Business Cards
8025 N. Division, Suite F
Spokane, WA 99208
800-745-9565
Fax 509-467-9572

Free Lance Writers/Newsletters,Magazines, Newspapers,Books

Howard Schneider
1109 del Nido Court
Ojai, CA 93023
805-646-8113
800-208-7046
Fax 805-640-8227

All About Books
Marilyn & Tom Ross
Box 1500-NSA
Buena Vista, CO 81211
800-548-1876

Appendix

Video/Audio Cassette Production & Duplication

P.C.S. Corporation
6211 South 380 West
Salt Lake City, Utah 84107
801-256-9393
Fax 801-263-1318
Preparation, duplication, printing, and package creation

Video/Audio Cassette Duplication
National Cassette Services, Inc.
613 Commerce Ave.
P.O. Box 99
Front Royal, VA 22630
703-635-4181
800-541-0551 East Coast
800-541-0661 West Coast
Fax 703-636-4240

Master Duplicating Corporation
2002 North 25th Drive
Phoenix, AZ 85009
602-269-2869
800-228-8919
Fax 602-484-7325

Cassette Works
125 N. Aspen Ave.
Azusa, CA 91702
818-969-6699
800-425-8273
Fax 818-969-6099

Magazines

Personal Selling Power
P.O. Box 5467
Fredericksburg, VA 22403-9904
800-752-7355
703-752-7000

Secrets of Personal Marketing Power

Sales & Marketing Management
Bill Communications, Inc.
355 Park Ave. South
New York, NY 10010-1789
800-821-6897

Sharing Ideas Newsmagazine
Royal Publishing, Inc.
P.O. Box 1120
Glendora, CA 91740
818-335-8069
Fax 818-335-6127

Miscellaneous Directories/Media Reports

The National Directory of Catalogs
Oxbridge Communications, Inc.
202-741-0231

The Salesman's Guide
Directory of Corporate Meeting Planners
Directory of Association Meeting Planners
121 Chanlon Road
New Providence, NJ 07974
800-521-8110

Radio-TV Interview Report
Bradley Communications Corp.
135 E. Plumstead Ave., #707
Lansdowne, PA 19050
800-989-1400

Working Press of The Nation
121 Chanlon Road
New Providence, NJ 07974
800-521-8110
up-to-date information—over 28,000 media sources

Appendix

Writer's Digest
P.O. Box 2123
Harlan, Iowa 51593
800-333-0133

Broadcast Interview Source
Yearbook of Experts, Authorities, and Spokespersons
Mitchell P. Davis, Editor
2233 Wisconsin Ave N.W., #540
Washington, DC 20007-4104
Order Desk: 800-955-0311
202-333-4904
Fax 202-342-5411

Broadcast Interview Source
Talk Show Selects
Mitchell P. Davis, Editor
2233 Wisconsin Ave N. W.
Washington, D.C. 20007
Order Desk: 800-955-0311
202-333-4904
Fax 202-342-5411
A guide to the nation's most influential radio & TV talk shows

Broadcast Interview Source
Power Media Selects
Alan Caruba, Editor
2233 Wisconsin Ave. N. W.
Washington, D.C. 20007
Order Desk: 800-955-0311
202-333-4904
Fax 202-342-5411
Over 700 of the most influential print and broadcast media outlets

151

Secrets of Personal Marketing Power

Mailing List Company

Bocca Direct Marketing
P.O. Box 310
Manhattan Beach, CA 90266
310-546-2888 CA
617-331-0404 MA
800-356-5478

Book Publishers

Kendall/Hunt Publishing Company
4050 Westmark Drive
P.O. Box 1840
Dubuque, Iowa 52004-1840
319-589-1000

Book Printers

McNaughton & Gunn, Inc.
P.O. Box 10
Saline, Michigan 48176
313-429-5411
Fax 313-429-4033

Newsletter Information

Newsletters In Print Directory
Gale Research Inc.
835 Penobscot Building
Detroit, MI 48226
313-961-2242
Fax 313-961-6083

Hudsons Subscription Newsletter Directory
Newsletter Clearinghouse
44 West Market Street
P.O. Box 311
Rhinebeck, New York 12572

Appendix

Media/Public Relations

Media Relations
7850 Metro Parkway, Suite #206
Bloomington, Minnesota 55425
612-851-8711
Fax 612-851-8706

Associations (for book authors)

Publishers Marketing Association
2401 Pacific Coast Highway, Suite 102
Hermosa Beach, CA 90254
310-372-2732
Fax 310-374-3342

Networking/Lead Clubs

LeTip International
4926 Savannah St., Suite 175
San Diego, CA 92110
800-255-3847
619-275-0600
Fax 619-275-0681
over 400 Chapters nationwide

Ali Lassen's Leads Club
Box 279
Carlsbad, CA 92018
800-783-3761
619-434-3761
Fax 619-729-7792
300 Chapters Nationwide

153

Secrets of Personal Marketing Power

Books on Self Publishing

Para Publishing
Dan Poynter
P.O. Box 4232-P
Santa Barbara, CA 93140-4232
805 968-7277
800-727-2782
Fax 805-968-1379

Appendix

INDEX

A

Active listening 35
Advisory board 13
American Express 6, 7, 9
Articles 57, 62, 65, 66, 67, 74, 80
Artists 6, 109, 124, 127
Assets xi, 52, 137, 138
Association 13, 24, 34, 40, 44, 49,
    56, 58, 60, 61, 62, 72, 88, 101,
    102, 109, 114, 117, 137, 138,
    150, 153, 158
Athlete 6, 98, 128
Audio brochure 122, 123, 124
Audio newsletters &
    magazines 60, 61, 62
Authenticity 26
Author 6, 9, 10, 17, 18, 21, 29,
    36, 74, 76, 77, 79, 88, 98, 117,
    118, 124, 153
Authority 49, 55, 61, 65, 73, 81

B

Believing in yourself 5
Biggest traps 28
Biographical 67, 111
Blinders 29, 67
Boldly market 5
Bright future xii, 75
Build recognition 57
Burning desire 25
Business xi, xii, 35, 38, 39, 43,
    62, 72, 76, 77, 79, 80, 128, 129

Business growth xii, 65
Business owner xii
Business resource 6

C

Calendar announcement 111,
    113
Campaign 11, 12, 65, 75, 89, 114,
    139
Campaigning 123
Career xi, 44, 49, 65, 67, 76, 88,
    120, 126, 127
Celebrities 5, 76, 98, 137
Celebrity endorsement 9
Center of your power 7, 33, 34
Challenging marketplace xi
Change xi, 34, 38, 53, 81, 127,
    157
Characteristic traits 17, 101
Civic clubs 13, 40
Cliff-hanging 25
Commitment 25, 26, 27, 36, 135
Communication 34, 35, 37, 39,
    55, 100, 127
Compelling 73
Competitive xi, xii, 42, 44, 52,
    53, 60
Competitors 53, 128, 137
Computer technology 106
Conditioning 26, 27, 133
Consultant xii
Consumerism 52
Courage 129

155

Creative channels   62
Creative process   127
Creative vision   xii, 75
Credibility   7, 14, 35, 43, 55, 65,
   78
Customer   8, 12, 13, 14, 39, 43,
   44, 55, 57, 60, 61, 62, 80, 84,
   85, 86, 88, 96, 97, 100, 102,
   104, 105, 106, 107, 118, 119,
   120, 121, 123, 124, 125, 126,
   128, 129, 141
Customer base   55, 100, 104, 119
Customer mailing   128, 129

D

Dictator   6
Direct mail   93, 104, 107, 114,
   117, 119
Discriminate   42
Distinctive   12, 15
Dream(s)   xi, xii, 9, 10, 18, 20, 21,
   24, 25, 100, 144
Dreams into reality   19, 25

E

Education   6, 7, 17, 20, 52, 72, 75,
   78, 79, 103, 105, 106, 120, 122
Effectiveness   25, 95
Electronic media   75, 98, 99, 113,
   121, 139
Elusive secret   xi
Empower   28, 35, 45, 144
Endorsement(s)   5, 6, 9, 13, 98
Energy force   15
Enlightenment   xi
Enterprise   xii, 7, 125
Epitomize   18
Eternal flame   xii
Excellence   80, 120
Exclusive market   8
Excuses   20, 77, 133, 134, 135
Expert   47, 55, 65, 72, 73, 74, 76, 79
Exposure   66, 79, 86, 98, 99, 101,
   102, 109, 120

F

Fear   xii, 20, 36, 38, 39, 101
Financial benefit   27
Financial freedom   xii, 79
Financial rewards   xii
First impression   81
Follow-up   14, 40, 42, 43, 44, 84,
   97, 103, 112
Free publicity   75, 80, 98
Frightening statistic   14
Fund raiser   xii

G

Gangster   6
Genius   5
Goal(s)   3, 8, 14, 15, 17, 21, 23,
   24, 25, 26, 27, 28, 29, 34, 35,
   41, 44, 51, 57, 58, 61, 72, 84,
   88, 100, 101, 103, 105, 108,
   120, 123, 139, 144
Golden destination   xi
Golden rules   35
Gravity pull   24
Great leaders   6
Greater success   8, 124
Group presentations   37, 101
Guest speaker   76, 102, 103, 109

H

Habit   20, 24, 25, 26, 27, 35, 38,
   114
Happenstance   4
Happiness   xii
Harboring   20
Human action   50

I

Imagination   25, 27, 53, 62, 127,
   128, 129
Impatience   25
Influence   18, 34, 35, 37, 39, 49,
   50, 51, 80, 95, 96, 107, 108, 118

Appendix

Information xi, 34, 35, 36, 37, 39,
41, 44, 57, 58, 60, 61, 62, 66,
67, 72, 77, 78, 83, 127, 150
Information resource 35
Information superhighway 106
Inherent right 20
Innate sense 4
Innovation xi, 124, 127, 128, 129
Inroad 9
Insight xi, 9, 43, 74, 81, 94, 128,
135, 136
Insurance xii, 56
Insurmountable 25
Interview(s) 13, 60, 61, 62, 64,
67, 68, 72, 73, 74, 76, 80, 101,
103, 111, 113, 150, 151
Inventory 80, 136

J

Jockeying 19
Jungle 8

K

Know-how xi
Knowledge xi, 43, 49, 80, 81

L

Lead club 13, 34, 153
Lead generation system 79
Leading edge 122, 123
Liabilities 138
Life's adversities 18
Lobbying 123, 126

M

Magic power 49
Major corporations 7
Market conditions 11, 14, 26
Market dominance xii
Market presence 11
Marketing kit 67
Marketing maverick(s) 5, 62, 65,
72

Marketing niche 7
Marketing tools xii
Marketing weapon 50, 51, 55,
76, 80, 81, 83, 86, 100, 105,
114, 122, 123, 129
Mass volume 27
Massive action 8, 103
Maximize marketing 57
Membership 40, 58, 80
Mental image 25
Methodology 78
Miracle maker 17
Mobilize 7, 34
Monarch 6
Monograph 58, 78
Mortgage lending xii
Motivation 18
Musician(s) 6, 127

N

Narrowcasting 98
Networking channels xi
New technology 52
News article(s) 103
News articles(s) 65
Newsletter(s) 13, 14, 51, 55, 56,
57, 58, 59, 60, 61, 62, 63, 64,
65, 67, 68, 76, 80, 95, 96, 98,
101, 102, 103, 119, 148, 152
Normal channels 8

O

Obstacles xi
Offramps 28
Optimal xii, 65, 123
Optimism xii
Optimistic xi
Optimize opportunity xi
Out-marketing xii

P

Participation 26
Passion 14, 19, 20, 25, 135
Passionate xii, 128

Secrets of Personal Marketing Power

Perception   26, 81
Performance   40, 57, 65, 128
Performance goals   57
Permission request   58, 96
Persistence   14, 18, 19
Personal fitness trainer   xii
Personal Marketing Power   4, 6,
   7, 12, 13, 14, 15, 17, 18, 19, 21,
   24, 25, 27, 28, 34, 35, 36, 41,
   44, 45, 49, 65, 74, 88, 93, 95,
   97, 100, 109, 131, 144, 158
Personal vision   26
Personalized   13, 14, 42, 43, 86,
   125
Pessimist   18, 126
Pessimistic   xi
Photo business card(s)   13, 14,
   83, 84, 85, 86, 95, 120, 147
Photo post card(s)   86, 88, 89,
   111, 126, 148
Photograph   58, 67, 83, 111, 112
Plan of action   11, 21, 142
Planning   15, 17, 101
Politician   6
Politics   xii
Position yourself   8, 11, 12, 13,
   21, 27, 70, 73, 80
Positioning   11, 13, 19, 106
Positive mind set   xi
Positive response   36
Positive thinkers   5
Possibilities   27, 29, 84, 101, 127,
   128
Power group presentations   37
Power lift   15
Power networker   10, 36, 38, 40
Power of people   95
Power plan   131
Powers of influence   49
Pre-publication   87
Press release   57, 111, 112
Principles of influence   49, 50
Print media   68, 112, 113
Private screening   25
Proactivity   26, 27
Procrastination   xii, 24, 25, 93, 142

Professional life   10
Professional presence   xii, 40, 43,
   50, 65, 78, 81
Professional speaker   xii
Profitable   21, 44, 79, 80, 104
Program   12, 34, 40, 60, 61, 68,
   74, 75, 77, 80, 98, 99, 102, 103,
   106, 108, 113, 121, 123, 124,
   125, 139
Promotional   13, 58, 66, 68, 84,
   88, 94, 101, 103, 121
Prospecting   79
Prosperous enterprise   xii
Provocation   34
Public relations   4, 75
Public service   111, 113
Publication   13, 59, 62, 66, 67, 87,
   113, 120, 126
Publicity   7, 75, 80, 98, 101, 112
Publishing   5, 6, 7, 58, 77, 150,
   152, 154

Q

Quantum jump   xii
Quantum leap   7

R

Real estate   xii, 56, 67, 76, 79, 84
Realize your dreams   24
Reciprocal   34
Reciprocity   40, 41, 49
Referral   11, 12, 14, 39, 40, 41, 43,
   44, 57, 80, 95, 96, 97, 103, 104
Referral card   96
Rejection   18, 38, 39
Relationship building   38
Relationship(s)   xi, 34, 38, 85, 86,
   108, 120, 125, 139, 144
Resources   12, 28, 40, 41, 52,
   77, 81, 95, 137, 138, 140, 145,
   147
Restructuring   28
Rightsizing   28
Rule of Success   106

158

Appendix

S

Sabotage   24
Sales   7, 39, 52, 55, 56, 61, 65, 67, 69, 72, 73, 76, 78, 80, 83, 86, 87, 88, 94, 95, 98, 104, 105, 121, 123, 126, 150
Salespeople   6
Savvy   34, 39, 41, 42, 65, 89, 120, 124
Secret weapon   51
Secrets   xii, 34, 45, 74
Self-assessment   26
Self-confidence   17, 81
Self-esteem   17
Self-fulfilling prophecy   26
Self-imposed   xi
Self-promote   12, 89
Self-published   77, 79, 95
Seminar(s)   13, 17, 35, 36, 41, 42, 43, 57, 58, 60, 64, 66, 69, 76, 79, 88, 94, 95, 104, 105, 106, 107, 109, 113, 114, 117, 119, 123, 124, 126, 129, 139
Simple truth   93
Smart Action Step   14
Smart decision   14, 43, 118
Smart questions   36, 37, 118
Social activist   xii
Speaking to groups   99, 100, 101
Special magic   81
Spirit of giving   10
Strategic   13, 124
Strategies   xii, 58, 61, 74, 81, 86
Success   xi, xii, 35, 38, 44, 64, 73, 74, 75, 78, 82, 86, 88, 124, 129, 158
Successful path   7
Sudden leap to success   8
Synergy   34, 45, 144

T

Tactical campaign   11, 12
Talent   18, 19, 20, 80

Talk show   72, 74, 75, 103, 109, 113, 151
Targeted market   56, 103
Teaching   78, 79, 80
Team marketing   124
Technology   34, 39, 52, 106
Ten Commandments   144
Tendencies   24
Testimonials   5, 14, 57, 94, 110, 117, 121
Thank you(s)   19, 40, 41, 42, 43, 85, 86, 89, 97, 108, 109
Thinking positively   5
Trade show   13, 122
Traditional attitudes   4
Traditional boundaries   84
Traditional wisdom   17, 18

U

Unique   85
Unsavory people   41
Unsolicited   117, 118, 119

V

Valued Customer Card   85, 86
Video brochure   121, 122, 123
Visibility   39, 40, 41, 42, 43, 44, 50, 51, 55, 66, 84, 100, 125
Vision   9, 10, 24, 25, 26, 27, 28, 29, 44, 67, 75, 109, 124, 128, 135, 136, 144

W

Wealthy   xi, 64, 79, 133
Wisdom   xi
Wizardry   63
Working hard   xi
Working harder   5
Workshop   13, 95, 104, 105, 106, 107, 109, 114, 123, 124, 139
Writer   xii

Secrets of Personal Marketing Power

"PEOPLE TALK ABOUT DON'S SEMINARS"

EXCERPTS FROM SOME OF THE HUNDREDS OF LETTERS DON PRICE RECEIVES FROM SEMINAR ATTENDEES

"I found your comments insightful and on the leading edge of the industry. I left with a wealth of ideas and information for myself and direction for the company."
Jammaal Wilkes—Los Angeles, CA

"I have attended many seminars and I must say yours was the best. I would recommend your seminar to any new, struggling or underachieving salesperson in any industry who needs fresh ideas."
Douglas Taylor—Totowa, NJ

"I can't tell you how glad I am that I was exposed to your seminar and learning materials so early in my career. I know I will possess countless advantages over my competitors thanks to you."
Tara Duckworth—Roseville, CA

"I really enjoyed your seminar. You helped remind me not to just sit back and take my business for granted. Thank you for sharing your knowledge and enthusiasm."
Fran Warner—Memphis, TN

"Today's seminar was great!! I found it highly motivating. I just wanted to hurry back to my office to sell, sell, sell."
Sandra Berg—Englewood Cliffs, NJ

Appendix

"Your Seminar was great!! I cannot tell you what a positive impact your seminar had on my co-workers and myself. It will change the way I look at my career."
Bill Slobin—Farmington, MI

"Your message was thought-provoking and it gave me inspiration to continue in the field of Real Estate Finance."
Gwendolyn Ross—Pasadena, CA

"I appreciated your excellent presentation. Your seminar poked my creative mind—for I learned many successful marketing tips."
R. Michael Lennox—Scottsdale, AZ

"Thank you, thank you, thank you for your seminar this morning. This was my second time attending in the last two months. You gave me an answer for my advertising, and some direction for the future. I will continue to recommend your seminars to my friends and associates."
Beverly Carroll—Granada Hills, CA

Secrets of Personal Marketing Power

For Those Needing Help

Don L. Price is a widely recognized speaker on "Personal Marketing Power." Don's programs are well-known for their innovative, creative and powerful ideas. His unparalleled messages of personal power, productivity and success will undoubtedly prove beneficial to the success of individuals, organizations, and associations.

For further information about his programs, please contact:

Don L. Price
P.O. Box 7000-700
Redondo Beach, CA 90277
310-379-7797